Glasgow, Scotland, UK

Travel

Author
Ethan Brown.

Publisher:
SONIT
2162 Davenport House
2162 Davenport House, 261 Bolton Road. Bury. Lancashire. BL8 2NZ. United Kingdom.

Table of Content

Summary

Travel makes one modest. You got to realize that the world is so big and see what a tiny place you occupy in the world.

With people, their culture, thoughts and ideas also travel. When they go from one place to the other, they are bound to meet people and share their thoughts and experiences with them. This is where exchange of ideas takes place, and it definitely broadens a person's outlook. It makes him/her think in a different way, from a different perspective. When we speak of cultural influences and exchange, food is one of the important factors. The food habits of people say a lot of things about them. It is very interesting to discover new and unknown ways and values; they really add spice to life.

Traveling also creates lifelong memories. Whether a person travels solo or with family and friends, the experience definitely gives him/her nice and exciting stories, which he/she can share with people back home. A good long holiday with loved ones enables him/her to spend some quality time with them, which in turn, helps to renew and restore relationships and creates very strong one-to-one and family bonds. In fact, traveling away from home and spending time with near and dear one(s) can give the relationship an entirely new perspective and possibly, people may start understanding each other in a better way.

Above all, traveling and getting away from our homes enables us to spend some time with our own selves. It makes us more sensitive and more tolerant towards others. It makes it easier for us to meet and mingle with different kinds of people, and also teaches us to live life to the fullest

Introduction

Glasgow is the biggest city in Scotland, with a population of about 600,000 in the city itself, or over 2 million if the surrounding towns of the Clydeside conurbation are taken into account. Located at the west end of Scotland's Central Belt on the banks of the River Clyde, Glasgow's historical importance as Scotland's main industrial centre has been challenged by decades of change and various regeneration efforts. The third largest city in the entire United Kingdom (by population), it remains one of the nation's key economic centres outside London.

In recent years, Glasgow has been awarded the European titles of City of Culture (1990), City of Architecture and Design (1999) and Capital of Sport (2003). In 2008, Glasgow became the second Scottish city to join the UNESCO Creative Citiesinitiative when it was named as a UNESCO City of Music (joining Bologna and Seville). In preparing its bid, Glasgow counted an average of 130 music events a week ranging from pop and rock to Celtic music and opera.

The city has transformed itself from being the once mighty powerhouse of industrial Britain to a centre for commerce, tourism, and culture. Glasgow was the host city for the Commonwealth Games in 2014.

Glasgow has become one of the most visited cities in the British Isles, and visitors will find a revitalised city centre, the best shopping outside London without a doubt, excellent parks and museums (most of which are free), and easy access to the Highlands and Islands.

Defining Glasgow

The term "Glasgow" in itself can be ambiguous. Various boundary changes over the years have blurred the distinction between the actual *City of Glasgow*administrative area, and *Greater Glasgow*; the contiguous metropolitan area which occupies much of the lower Clyde Valley with the city itself at its core, and surrounding burghs such as Rutherglen, Bearsden, Milngavie and Clydebank, all of which still fall under the Glasgow postcode area and 0141 telephone code. Residents of these areas are often still fiercely defensive of their home towns and may or may not identify themselves as "Glaswegian", but since many of the city's attractions fall within these areas, for the tourist, they may be considered one and the same.

Dialect

The speed of the conversation tends to be quite quick in Glasgow. If necessary, ask people to repeat (even slowly!) what they are saying, Glaswegians are generally very friendly and able to communicate in far more formal English than that which is commonly used if it is required. Standing on a city centre street corner with a map in the daytime is usually a cue for passing Glaswegians to offer help in finding your way.

As with all areas of Scotland, regional dialects are present in Glasgow. The Glaswegian dialect of Scots or "patter" as the more jovial version of it is known, has evolved over the history of the city. As each wave of migration takes place, new words and phrases are added to the Glaswegian "patter". There is a strong Celtic language connection due to the Lowland Scots, Highland Gaelic and Irish Gaelic influences.

Orientation

For the visitor, central Glasgow can be divided into two main areas, the City Centre, which contains the majority of tourist sights and much of the city's shopping and entertainment, as well as its commercial heart, and the West End, the bohemian area of cafés, restaurants and bars surrounding the University of Glasgow and Kelvingrove Museum. The best way to get good vistas of the city is to climb the many "drumlins" (hills) upon which the central area is built.

Outside of central Glasgow, the East End lies east of the City Centre centred along Gallowgate and London Road. The South Side contains the neighbourhoods that lie to the south of the River Clyde, while the North Side is the area north of central Glasgow. Along the banks of the River Clyde west of the City Centre is an old industrial area which is in the process of regeneration and contains many new and impressive structures, such as the Clyde Auditorium, the Science Centre and the Riverside Museum.

City Centre

The City Centre (known as "town" or "the toon" to locals) is bounded by the M8 motorway to the north and west, High Street to the east, and the River Clyde to the south. This is the area where most visitors will start, and the most notable elements are the grid plan of streets and the lavish Victorian and Edwardian buildings and civic squares which give the area much of its character. The main arteries of the City Centre are Argyle Street and Sauchiehall Street which both run on an east-west axis. They are linked by Buchanan Street which runs north-south. Together, these three streets form the main shopping thoroughfares.

The eastern side of the City Centre is a sub-district known as Merchant City, which contains Glasgow's original medieval core, centred around the Glasgow Cross (the junction of Trongate, Saltmarket, High Street, Gallowgate and London Road). Merchant City extends up to George Square, with many ornate buildings that date back to Glasgow's emergence as an industrial city. High Street north of the Glasgow Cross is the main artery of Old Glasgow and leads uphill to the Glasgow Cathedral and the Necropolis cemetery.

The western area of the City Centre contains the city's core commercial and business district and is dominated by Blythswood Hill, which is centred around Blythswood Square. Running parallel to Sauchiehall Street, Bath Street is the main route into the neighbourhood and has a rich mix of independent shops and bars, as well as distinctive Georgian town house style architecture. South of Blythswood Hill is the city's financial district, with many modern glass and steel office buildings which stand alongside their classical counterparts. Further south, on the north bank of the River Clyde is the district of Anderston, formerly a dockland area, badly scarred by the city's industrial decline and the urban regeneration schemes of the 1960s but now being redeveloped as a residential and commercial area.

West End

To the west of the City Centre, no official definition of where the West End boundary line exists, but it can roughly be defined as being bounded by the M8 motorway to the east, Great Western Road to the north, the River Clyde to the South and Crow Road to the west. The nucleus of the area is undoubtedly the neo-Gothic University of Glasgow, which acts as the anchor for this bohemian district, with its lovely architecture, tree lined streets and quaint shopping areas.

The primary east-west artery is Argyle Street/Dumbarton Road, while Byres Road is the main north-south artery and contains a number of independent shops, bars and restaurants. Ashton Lane connects Byres Road to the University campus and is a cobbled backstreet with distinctive whitewashed buildings, holding an eclectic mix of bars and eateries that make it a tourist hotspot (be careful as the Lane can be a bit of a tourist trap during the summer months when the students of the university are not there to keep the bar prices reasonable). To the east of the university campus and just downhill is Kelvingrove Park, with the tree-lined Kelvin Way as the main avenue through the park, which connects with Argyle Street near the Kelvingrove Museum.

Short History of Glasgow

Glasgow was probably founded in the 6th century when St Mungo built a church at place called Glas Gu. (It means green place). A fishing settlement at the green place eventually grew into a small town. Glasgow was given a bishop in 1115, indicating it was a fairly important settlement by that time.

The church in Glasgow was replaced by a cathedral in 1136. The cathedral burned in 1172 but it was rebuilt. Then in the years 1175-78 (the exact date is not known) the king gave Glasgow a charter. (A charter was a document granting the townspeople certain rights).

In the Middle Ages Glasgow had a weekly market. From 1190 it also had a fair, which was held each July. In the Middle Ages a fair was like a market but it was held only once a year and people would come from a wide area to buy and sell at one. In Glasgow there were many craftsmen including butchers and bakers. There were also skinners, tanners and glovers (leather glove makers) in Glasgow as well as fullers (men who cleaned and thickened wool by pounding it in a mixture of water and clay) and dyers. There were also many fishermen in Glasgow.

Medieval Glasgow probably had a population of about 1,500. That seems very small to us but in the Middle Ages towns were much smaller than they are today. Even so in the Middle Ages Glasgow was not one of Scotland's larger or more important towns. One reason for this is that Glasgow was on the wrong side of Scotland to trade with European countries such as Germany, Belgium, Holland and the Scandinavian countries. Furthermore Glasgow competed with other towns on the Clyde (Dumbarton, Rutherglen and Renfrew). The little town of Glasgow only consisted of 4 main streets laid out in a cross.

Yet Dominican friars (known as black friars because of the color of their costumes) came to Glasgow in 1260. The friars were like monks and took vows of chastity and poverty but instead of withdrawing from society they went out to preach. There were also hospitals in Glasgow run by the Church. In them monks would care for the sick as best they could. A hospital for lepers was founded south of the Clyde in 1350.

In the late Middle Ages Glasgow slowly grew more important. In 1410 the wooden bridge across the Clyde was replaced with a stone one. Glasgow did not have stone walls but it did have stone gates (the spaces between them were filled by houses). Then in 1491 the Bishop of Glasgow was granted the right to operate a public scales for weighing produce. It was called the Tron and it gave its name to the Trongate.

As a sign of its growing importance Glasgow in 1451 Glasgow was allowed to have a university . The Papal document that founded the university described Glasgow as a 'place of renown, where the air is mild and victuals are plentiful'. A grammar school was founded in Glasgow in 1460.

Meanwhile in 1454 Glasgow was made a royal burgh. Then in 1492 Glasgow was given an archbishop.

In the early Middle Ages there was one general market in Glasgow but as the town grew separate markets were held. By the late 15th century there was a salt market (which lives on as a place name). There was also a wool and linen market about the market cross. A fruit and vegetable market was held in Gallowgate. There was also a meat market just north of

Trongate, a fish market at Westport, and a horse market and a grain market by the High Street.

Glasgow in the 16th Century and 17th Century

In 1526 Archbishop Blackadder founded another hospital in Glasgow. However Glasgow was besieged several times during the 16th century in 1516, 1517, 1544, 1560, 1568 and 1570. During these sieges cannon damaged the castle.

Yet Glasgow grew rapidly during this era. By the 1600 century Glasgow probably had a population of 7,000. By the 1700 it was about 12,000. In 1626 a new tollbooth was built. It was demolished in 1812 except for the steeple. In 1649 a writer called Glasgow 'one of the most considerable burghs of Scotland as well for buildings as for the trade'. Hutchesons 'hospital' for old men and orphans opened in 1650.

However plague struck Glasgow in 1646. There was also a disastrous fire in Glasgow in 1652 and another fire in 1677. However each time the plague struck Glasgow recovered and it continued to grow and prosper.

The Merchant's House where merchants met to talk shop was built in 1659. The building was demolished in 1817 except for the steeple which lives on as the merchant's steeple.

By the late 17th century there were several industries in Glasgow including, soap boiling, sugar processing, rope making, glass making, cloth making and porcelain making. There were also factories where candles were made. Meanwhile the first quay was built at Broomielaw in 1601. It was rebuilt several times during the 17th and 18th centuries. In 1668 the town council purchased land further along the Clyde. They built quays and warehouses there and Port Glasgow came into being.

In 1674 the first cargo of tobacco arrived in Glasgow. It soon became one of Glasgow's most important imports. Once colonies were founded in North America and the West Indies Glasgow benefited from its position on the west of Scotland.

However Glasgow, like all towns at that time, was dirty and unsanitary. Some attempt was made to improve things in 1685 when the authorities forbade people to leave piles of dung outside their houses. (There was, of course, a great deal of horse dung as well as dung from animals on their way to market or the slaughterhouse).

Glasgow in the 18th Century

By the beginning of the 18th century Glasgow probably had a population of about 12,000 and it grew rapidly. By the end of the century the population of Glasgow had reached 84,000. By the standards of the time it was a large town.

In the 1720's Daniel Defoe described Glasgow: 'Glasgow is, indeed, a very fine city, the four principal streets are the fairest for breadth, and the finest built that I have ever seen in one city together. The houses are all of stone and generally equal and uniform in height'. He also said 'It is the cleanest and most beautiful, and best city in Britain, London excepted'.

As Glasgow grew new streets were laid out. In the 1720s Candleriggs and King Street were built. In 1751 the West Port or gate was demolished and the main obstacle to westward growth was removed. Virginia Street was built in 1753 and Jamaica Street was built in 1763. Queen Street followed in 1777 and St Enochs Square in 1783. Buchanan Street was built in 1786 and St Georges Square in 1787. In the 1790s Hutcheson Street and Glassford Street were built. During the 18th century a new suburb grew up at the Gorbals. Meanwhile Pollock House was built in 1752. The Royal Exchange was built in 1775. A second bridge over the Clyde was built in 1772.

In the 18th century Glasgow was famous for its fine linen. In the late 18th century cotton spinning became a major industry in Glasgow. Meanwhile Glasgow gained its first newspaper in 1715. Pollok House was built about 1752. It was given to the city in 1966. A second bridge over the Clyde was built in 1772 and the castle was finally demolished in 1792. Glasgow gained its first (not very effective) police force in 1788 and the Royal Infirmary was built in 1794. Meanwhile the Monkland Canal opened in 1793.

Glasgow in the 19th Century

In the 19th century Glasgow continued to grow very rapidly. By 1871 it had reached a population of half a million. This was despite a very high infant mortality rate. (Up to half of all children born died before their 5th birthday). Poor people in Glasgow lived in dreadfully overcrowded conditions. Most of them lived in one or two rooms in tenements.

Meanwhile the Nelson Monument was built in 1806. The first museum in Glasgow, the Hunterian, opened in 1807. It is named after Dr William Hunter who left his collection to the university in 1783.

The Botanic Gardens were laid out in 1817. Also that year St Andrews the Roman Catholic Cathedral in Glasgow was built. Argyle Arcade was built in 1827. Necropolis cemetery was laid out in 1833. Many rich merchants were buried there in elaborate tombs.

Glasgow Green was laid out as a park between 1815 and 1826. Kelvingrove Park was laid out in 1852. In 1862 Queens Park opened. Alexandra Park followed in 1870.Meanwhile the Custom House was built in 1840. St Georges Cross was built in 1837. A Corn Exchange where grain was bought and sold was built in Hope Street in 1843 and Glasgow School of Art was founded in 1845. The Athenaeum was built in 1847. Glasgow Academy was formed in 1846.

Caledonia Road Church was built in 1857 but burned in 1965. St Vincent Street Church was built in 1859 by Alexander Thomson (1817-1875). Great Western Terrace was built in 1870.

Many more buildings were erected in Glasgow in the 19th century. The Stock Exchange was built in Buchanan Street in

1875. Also in 1875 the Fish Market was built. Mitchell Library was built in 1877. The City Chambers were built in 1888. Queens Cross Church was built in 1897 by Charles Rennie Mackintosh (1868-1928). The same man also built the Glasgow School of Art Building in 1909.

Transport also improved in Victorian Glasgow. In 1845 the first horse drawn buses began running in Glasgow. From 1872 they were replaced by horse drawn trams. After 1898 the trams changed to electricity. (The first electricity generating station in Glasgow was built in 1893). Queen Street station was built in 1842. Buchanan Street station was built in 1849. Central station followed in 1879. Glasgow gained an underground railway in 1896.

In the mid-19th century Glasgow was described as 'possibly the filthiest and unhealthiest of all the British towns'. There were outbreaks of cholera in Glasgow in 1849 and in 1854. The first time 3,777 people died. The second time 3,885 died.

But conditions in Glasgow improved in the later 19th century. In 1859 Glasgow gained a piped water supply. In 1893 the first electric streetlights were switched on in Glasgow but they only slowly replaced gas. Also in the late 19th century a network of sewers was built in Glasgow.

Furthermore the Albert Bridge was built in 1871. A pedestrian tunnel under the Clyde was built in 1895. In 1898 the Peoples Palace opened on Glasgow Green.

Major industries in Glasgow in the 19th century included shipbuilding, Cotton, engineering, carpet making, pottery and glass. In the late 19th century the port's facilities were greatly improved by building docks and new quays. The tonnage of ships built in the city rose from 20,000 in the year 1850 to 5000,000 in 1900. In 1888 an International Exhibition of Science and Art was held in Glasgow.

Glasgow in the 20th Century

In the 20th century amenities in Glasgow continued to improve. Kelvingrove art gallery opened in 1901. The Kings Theatre in Bath Street was built in 1904. However in the 1930s Glasgow suffered severe unemployment. Shipbuilding was one of the industries hardest hit by the depression, although it revived with the coming of the Second World War. On the other hand the first serious slum clearance in Glasgow began in the 1930s and in

1938 the Empire Exhibition was held on the site of Bellahouston Park.

During the Second World War Glasgow suffered from German bombing along with other towns in Clydeside. However, Glasgow escaped severe damage.

From the 1950s employment in Glasgow changed. In the 1930s most jobs were in manufacturing but in the 1960s and 1970s the situation changed so that most jobs were in service industries.

In the 1960s and 1970s, like many cities, Glasgow embarked on a program of slum clearance. Large areas of the central city like Gorbals were demolished. Some people were re-housed in flats. Others were re-housed in 'overspill' towns such as Glenrothes, Irvine, East Kilbride, Cumbernauld and Livingstone.

Other houses were demolished to make way for the M8 motorway. The last trams in Glasgow ran in 1962. In 1965 a road tunnel under the Clyde was built. In 1970 Kingston Bridge was built.

Also in 1970 Glasgow's Central Mosque was built. Meanwhile Strathclyde University was formed in 1964.

In the last part of the 20th century Glasgow turned to art and its heritage to attract visitors and provide jobs. The Hunterian Art Gallery opened in 1980. In 1983 the Burrell Collection went on display in a museum in the grounds of Pollock House. The Scottish Exhibition and Conference Centre was built in 1985. The Clyde Auditorium was added in 1997.

The McLellan galleries were severely damaged by fire in 1985. They were refurbished and reopened in 1990. Then the Gallery of Modern Art was built in 1996. Meanwhile in 1988 a Garden Festival was held in Glasgow. In 1990 it was made a European city of culture. Also in 1990 the Royal Concert Hall was opened. In 1996 a Festival of Visual Arts was held in the city. In 1999 Glasgow was designated the UK city of architecture and design.

In the 1980s and 1990s the traditional manufacturing industries of Glasgow went into a steep decline but the service industries grew. Industries such as retail, finance and tourism flourished. Glasgow School Museum of Education opened in 1990 and St Mungos Museum of Religious Life and Art opened in 1993. Buchanan Galleries Shopping Centre was built in 1999 and the Clyde Maritime Centre opened the same year.

Glasgow in the 21st Century

In the early 21st century Glasgow flourished. The IMAX cinema opened in 2000 and the Clyde Arc Bridge opened in 2006. Today the population of Glasgow is 598,000.

Travel and Tousim

Guide

Getting in

By plane

Glasgow is served by two main airports close to the city, which are Glasgow International Airport and Glasgow Prestwick International Airport. Edinburgh Airport is approximately 40 miles away.

Glasgow International Airport

(IATA: GLA). Located 8 miles west of the centre of Glasgow near the towns of Paisley and Renfrew, this is the city's principal airport, and the main direct long haul and transatlantic entry airport into Scotland. There are regular scheduled UK and European destinations, holiday charters, and the airport is the hub for the Scottish island network operated by Loganair. United Airlines operate a daily service from New York (Newark), while Emirates operate 2 daily flights from Dubai. If you are entering the United Kingdom via London, British Airways operates frequent shuttle flights to Glasgow Airport throughout the day from both Heathrow and Gatwick. British Airways also operates a regular business shuttle from London City Airport, although it can be considerably more expensive than flying from Heathrow or Gatwick. Cheaper fares are sometimes available if you book via a price comparison site, rather than going to BA direct. Alternatively, KLM flies regularly to Glasgow from Amsterdam-Schiphol, which connects with a wide range of international destinations. EasyJet flies from Luton, Stansted and Gatwick, and Ryanair flies from Dublin, Stansted and a number of Eastern European destinations.

The frequent Glasgow Shuttle bus departs from outside the terminal building to the city centre, dropping off near both main railway stations (£8.00 single, £12 open return). Slower, less frequent, but cheaper is First's route 747 (£4 single, £5 return).

The slowest, but cheapest, option is to use McGill's local bus 66 operating as often as every 10 min to Paisley Gilmour Street train station, where regular trains run to Glasgow Central in as little as ten minutes. Travelling to the airport you can buy an inclusive train and bus ticket from any train station: just ask for Glasgow

Airport and show the bus driver your train ticket. Travelling from the airport buy a coupon for £1.50 from the SPT Travel Information counter beside domestic arrivals, show it to the driver and then and use it for £1.50 of cr towards onward train travel from Paisley Gilmour Street station. A single from Glasgow Central to/from the airport costs £3.20, or £1.80 with a National Rail railcard.

Glasgow International Airport has 2 terminals. All passengers arrive in the first terminal arrivals hall. The first terminal is used for Thomson, Emirates, Jet2, Iberia and many more. Terminal 2 is only used for check in for Thomas Cook, Aer Lingus, Canadian Affair and Virgin. Glasgow Airport also has 2 prayer rooms: one in the second set of departure gates and the other in the arrivals hall. Be aware that there are 3 customs "channels." The blue channel is for EU arrivals, EEA Countries and Switzerland. All other nationals should enter through the green channel. The airport generally never gets overcrowded except at check-in and security.

Car parks serving Glasgow Airport

Address	On/Off Airport	Distance / Transfer Time	Security	Park Mark® Award	Additional Information

Airparks Glasgow	Burnbrae Drive, Linwood, Paisley, PA3 3BJ.	Off	-	High-fencing, floodlights, 24-hour CCTV and security patrols	Yes	Trailers are permitted within this car park at Glasgow but an extra space will be charged
Glasgow Long Stay	Glasgow Long Stay Supersaver, Arran Avenue, Glasgow Airport, Paisley, PA3 2AY.	On	10 minutes	24 hours a day, has 24-hour CCTV, and is fully fenced and floodlit	Yes	There are parking bays for Blue Badge holders near the bus stops. The courtesy coaches are wheelchair accessible and DDA compliant

Glasgow Prestwick International Airport

(IATA: PIK). This is about 50 km south west of Glasgow on the Ayrshire coast, is the city's secondary airport and a hub for Ryanair (see Discount airlines in Europe). Ryanair flies into Prestwick from a variety of Merranean resorts, which are mostly seasonal.

The airport has its own railway station, with two trains per hour to Glasgow Central (show your flight paperwork to get a £3.55 half price ticket; the journey takes around 45min). All trains from Ayr call at the airport. The A77/M77 roads run directly from Prestwick into the centre of Glasgow if you intend to drive.

The X77 bus also runs from the airport to Buchanan Bus Station throughout the day, and crucially covers the times (early morning and late evening) when the trains are not running.

Edinburgh International Airport

(IATA: EDI). Although not an immediately obvious choice, the capital's airport is easily accessible from Glasgow since it is on the western edge of Edinburgh, approximately 60km away and about an hours drive via the M8 motorway. Useful as both Ryanair and Easyjet have a number of European routes that are not available from either Glasgow International or Prestwick.

The airport is linked to Glasgow by Citylink buses twenty-four hours a day. A direct Citylink Air bus service runs from the airport to Buchanan Bus Station approximately every 30 minutes during the day, with the N900 bus serving the airport hourly during the night. Glasgow can also easily be reached from the airport via a connecting tram or bus to Haymarket railway station - all trains from Glasgow call here. See the main Edinburgh article for more details.

By train

Glasgow has two main line railway stations. Trains from the south of Scotland, the city's southern suburbs and all long distance trains from England arrive at Central Station (officially known as Glasgow Central), while shuttle trains from Edinburgh and anywhere north of Glasgow arrive at Queen Street Station.

Both stations are divided into a "High Level" (for main line inter-city services) and a subterranean "Low Level" (for local suburban services) - you will see this distinction being mentioned in timetables.

Both Central and Queen Street stations have left luggage lockers. The stations are an easy ten minute walk apart and the route is well signposted, or there's a frequent shuttle bus between them, which is free if you are holding a through railway ticket otherwise a fare of 50p is charged if you don't.

Most trains within Scotland are run by ScotRail.

From Edinburgh

Confusingly, there are four rail routes between the capital and Glasgow's two main line terminals. An off-peak return is around £11.50, regardless which route you use, a peak return is around £20. In summary the four routes are as follows - all depart from both Waverley and Haymarket stations:

Fastest: The *ScotRail Shuttle* via Falkirk High into Queen Street (High Level) - every 15 min on weekdays and Saturdays until 19:15, half hourly outside these times. Journey time 50 min.

Faster: *CrossCountry* or *Virgin Trains East Coast* trains via Motherwell into Central (High Level) - trains originating from Penzance, Plymouth, Bristol, Birmingham or London King's Cross make the journey at sporadic intervals throughout the day - journey time approx 1 hour. CrossCountry services have the cheapest walk-up one way fare between the two cities, of £7.50 for an Anytime single.

Slow: *ScotRail* services via Bathgate and Airdrie into Queen Street (Low Level) en route to Milngavie or Helensburgh Central - 4 trains per hour on weekdays & Saturdays until 18:30, half hourly outside these times. Journey time between 60-80 minutes. ScotRail normally recommend that travellers use this route if there is major disruption to the main shuttle service or to relieve pressure on it if large passenger numbers are expected due to events being held in either city.

Very Slow: *ScotRail* services via Shotts or Carstairs and Motherwell into Central (High Level) - every hour, journey time between 65-90min

From London and the South

Glasgow can be reached from London by either the West Coast or East Coast main lines. The quality and reliability of the rail services has improved a lot over the years, and it can be cheaper and almost as fast as flying once the time spent travelling to airports with their associated security hassles is taken into account.

Faster: Virgin Trains run 13 trains a day from London Euston via the West Coast route. Journey time is 4h30, with one northbound express completing the 400 mile journey in just over 4 hours. Prices Jan 2014: Single one-way fares £21.00 is booked up to 12 weeks in advance, rising to £59. Open off-peak return £130. Virgin also operate a two-hourly service from Birmingham.

Slower: Virgin Trains East Coast run 1 direct train a day from London King's Cross to Glasgow Central via the East Coast route (taking in York and Newcastle also). East Coast also operate a roughly hourly service from London to Edinburgh throughout the day, which connects with the Shuttle (see above). Journey time 5h45-6h30 (if connecting at Edinburgh). Single one-way fares start at £21.00 one way if booked on-line and up to 12 weeks in advance. Open off-peak returns are the same as for Virgin Trains.

Overnight: The Caledonian Sleeper is an overnight sleeper train that runs every night except Saturday to/from London Euston via the West Coast route. The journey takes approximately 8 hours, although is deliberately scheduled for a late departure and a reasonable arrival time. Tickets can be booked in the usual manner at any main line railway station in Britain or on-line: the cost of a return journey from London to Glasgow varies from around £100 for two one-way "Advance" tickets rising to the full open return fare of £165 (being the basic fare plus the cost of the sleeping berth in a compartment with either one or two beds). You can also travel in a seated carriage for around £23 one-way or £95 return (full fare). Certain BritRail passes can be used to buy tickets on the Sleeper trains, but supplements are payable for the berth: check before leaving your home country. The best value fares on the sleeper are inclusive (travel and berth) one-way tickets known as "Bargain Berths" available and are sold in limited numbers for £19, £29, £39 or £49 depending on how far in advance you book. It is occasionally possible to find "Bargain Berths" to/from Dalmuir (a suburb of Glasgow) after they have sold out to/from Glasgow Central. Solo travellers may have to share the sleeping compartment with a stranger of the same gender.

Within Scotland

Apart from the Edinburgh shuttles, the key inter-city rail routes to Glasgow from elsewhere in Scotland are as follows:

- ➢ Aberdeen and Dundee (via Perth): Hourly into Queen Street (High Level) throughout the day.

- ➢ Inverness (via Perth): Every two hours into Queen Street (High Level) throughout the day

- ➢ Stirling: Half Hourly (approximately) into Queen Street (High Level) throughout the day.

- ➢ Oban, Fort William and Mallaig via the West Highland Railway: Up to four trains per day into Queen Street (High Level). In addition, the overnight sleeper train from Fort William to London Euston calls at Queen Street (Low Level) to let off passengers in the late evening.

- ➢ Stranraer: Four trains per day into Central (High Level).

- ➢ Ayr (via Prestwick Airport, Troon and Kilwinning): Half Hourly into Central (High Level).

Other Rail Services

All national inter-city routes operate into Central (High Level).

Virgin Trains operate direct services to/from Birmingham New Street.

First Transpennine Express operate a direct service to Glasgow from Manchester Airport and Manchester Piccadilly.

CrossCountry operate a handful of early morning and late evening trains to/from the South West of England via Edinburgh, Newcastle, York, Sheffield, Birmingham New Street and Bristol.

By car

The main approaches to Glasgow are:

➢ from England on the M74 motorway; Glasgow is about 150km north of the border

➢ from Edinburgh (east) or Glasgow Airport (west) on the M8 motorway

➢ from Stirling and all points north and east on the M80 motorway

➢ from the Highlands on the A82 road

In 2011 the M74 Extension was completed, allowing an alternative route into the city centre via the south side. As of June 2013, many GPS services still do not recognise the new route, so bear this in mind if using sat-nav to navigate your way into the city!

Parking

On-street parking in the both the City Centre and West End is limited and expensive, metered bays are available at the side of the road and you pay at an adjacent machine and display a ticket in your windscreen or dashboard. The prices are typically £0.30-0.40 (depending on location) for every 12 min. In general, parking charges are levied M-Sa (this INCLUDES public holidays) and free after 18:30 and all day Sundays. But always check what the controlled hours are - these are shown on the ticket machines themselves and on adjacent signs. If attempting to park on the free periods - get there as early as possible before the locals do. Some parking areas are for residents only - DON'T be tempted to use them as you run the risk of being towed away!

There are many multi-storey car parks in the city centre; they are clearly signposted into "East", "West", "North" and "South" zones on all the approaches into the central area with an electronic display showing how many spaces are left in each. They don't however differentiate between the expensive NCP ones and the cheaper ones inside shopping malls or run by the council.

Park and Ride facilities are limited in Glasgow. Three different Park and Ride facilities can be found on the subway network; at Bridge Street (159 spaces), Kelvinbridge (150 spaces) and Shields Road (800 spaces). The cost of parking at each of these locations is £5 per day, which includes a return subway ticket. For those who already have a Subway season or multi-journey ticket, the charge is £2.40 per day. Some of the suburban railway stations also have small car parks. A bus park-and-ride is due to open shortly near Hampden Park which allows easy access from junction 1A of the M74.

In general, driving in Glasgow's central area should be avoided if you are not a confident driver, as there are one way systems, bus lanes and pedestrian precincts. Glaswegians are not the most patient drivers in the world, and they particularly dislike hesitancy (taxi drivers being the worst culprits). Parking restrictions are strictly enforced, and vehicles parked illegally or in an obstructive manner will be towed away and the owner of the vehicle will be liable for a £150 release charge to recover it.

As of May 2012, the city has introduced licence plate recognition cameras and extra manned patrols on the bus lanes within the city centre, getting caught will incur a £30 fixed penalty!

If, however, you are confident enough to hire a car or require it to save money on your travel, all the major rental companies and some lesser ones are at the airport. You should book your car rental in advance to avoid disappointment and can do so from price comparison companies such as Glasgow Airport Car Hire. Visitors from the United States and Canada should note that car rental companies will allocate you a manual transmission car by default, unless you specifically ask for an automatic.

By bus

Virtually all long-distance, and some short-distance, buses serving Glasgow arrive at the Buchanan Bus Station (in the city centre, close to Buchanan Street and Queen Street train station).

National Express, Scottish Citylink and Megabus are the main long-haul coach operators serving Glasgow. Somewhat confusingly, Citylink and Megabus often combine and merge services, so you may be put on a Citylink bus when you hold a Megabus reservation and vice versa.

Citylink operate the 900 bus service from Edinburgh, which runs up to every 15 minutes during the day. Buses from Edinburgh operate twenty-four hours a day, seven days a week, with the night service also serving Edinburgh Airport.

Through bus and ferry tickets from Dublin, Derry and Belfast can be obtained through Scottish Citylink or National Express, in addition to Ulsterbus for the latter two. There are also direct buses to Glasgow from Eastern Europe (mostly Poland), these operators come and go.

Note that the station is huge and very confusing, so you might have to ask for directions.

Some short-distance buses, particularly those from Helensburgh and Balloch, terminate on Osbourne Street, near the St. Enoch Shopping Centre.

By ferry

From Ireland: P & O ferries from Larne and Stena Line ferries from the Port of Belfast operate to Cairnryan; six miles north of Stranraer and seventy-eight miles south of Glasgow. Cairnryan is linked to Stanraer by the 350 bus (which is timed to meet both the Belfast and Larne ferries), and thence by ScotRail train to Glasgow (a change of train may be required in Ayr). Alternatively, the 923 bus operates directly from Cairnryan to Glasgow.

Through train tickets are available from any railway station in the Republic of Irelandand Northern Ireland to Glasgow via the ferry to Cairnryan, with bus connections from Belfast to the port and Cairnryan to Stranraer included in the fare. Fares start at £25 one way (£16.50 with a railcard) for Belfast to Glasgow (available on the day of travel from most railway stations), taking about five hours. Similarly, Citylink sell inclusive coach and ferry tickets between Dublin, Derry, Belfast and Glasgow.

Getting around

Strathclyde Partnership for Transport (SPT) is the agency responsible for the local public transport network, which it describes as one of the most integrated and developed in the UK, not European standards. Nevertheless, Glasgow's public transport system is one of the most extensive in the UK outside of London.

On foot

The centre of Glasgow is very pedestrian-friendly with major shopping streets given over to foot traffic. As you move out of the city centre, all areas have proper pavements, and most major junctions have pedestrian crossings. The River Clyde also has several foot bridge crossings. The main difficulty with walking out of the centre of town is finding where the crossings over/under the M8 are. As you head west, some roads appear to go over Charing Cross only for the pavement to disappear. As you head north, the underpasses at Cowcaddens can sometimes feel unwelcoming.

Glasgow walking directions can be planned online with the walkit.com walking route planner.

By cycle

Glasgow now offers a cycle hire scheme, which covers the city centre and some of the inner suburbs. For an half-hourly charge (after registration), bicycles may be hired from automated hire stations around the city. The bikes can be unlocked and ridden around the city with a cr card, and must be returned to another hire station by locking the bike into the rack.

By subway

Glasgow's subway runs in a double circle around the Glasgow city centre and some inner suburbs. Contrary to what tourist guidebooks would have you believe, locals never call it the "Clockwork Orange" (that is a fantasy of the media) and most will refer to it simply as "the Subway". The system serves the city centre, the West End (around Glasgow University) and Ibrox Stadium. There are interchanges with surface trains at Buchanan

Street (linked to Queen Street) and Partick stations, with St Enoch being a short walk from Central.

The cost for a disposable ticket is £1.70 flat fare, £3.20 for two journeys or £4.10 for one day's unlimited travel. Those intending to stay in the city for a period of time or intend to visit regularly can purchase an anonymous Smartcard at any subway station for £3. Smartcard fares are £1.50 flat fare, with a £2.90 daily cap. Weekly, monthly, 6-monthly and yearly tickets are also available for Smartcard holders.

No bikes are allowed. As of 2018, wheelchairs are not conveyed on the Subway, however a modernisation program is underway so that wheelchair-users can travel between St. Enoch and Govan from 2020 onwards.

Trains generally run every 4-8min from 06:30-23:45 (Sunday 10:00-18:12).

By train

Suburban trains radiate from Central and Queen Street stations to the suburbs and surrounding towns. The network is the largest in the UK outside of London, although there are only two trains per hour on some routes; others are much more frequent.

Central serves the dense suburban network which sprawls throughout the southern suburbs of the city, as well as outer suburban services to the Inverclyde and Ayrshire coasts. The underground lower level platforms of both Central and Queen Street stations are hubs for the east-west electric network north of the river, which provide useful links to the West End (thus complementing the Subway) and further west to the northern Clyde coast towns of Dumbarton, Helensburgh and Balloch, the gateway to Loch Lomond and the Southern Highlands. More recently, the Low Level line from Queen Street has been extended eastwards to the West Lothian towns of Bathgate and Livingston.

Bikes go free, but many trains have no bike spaces. The SPT Day Tripper ticket (explained below) gives you complete freedom of the network, and the Roundabout ticket (also explained below) gives off-peak freedom of the suburban train network within the city boundary only as well as the Subway.

By bus

Buses go everywhere. First Glasgow is the main operator within the city boundary. There is a bus at least every 10min on main routes during the day, making it easy to get into the centre of town, though getting out to a specific destination less easy. However, services on many routes are much less frequent in the evening. In the city centre, buses do not always stop at every stop on their route, so check the sign at the stop. Stops are clearly marked with the services that stop there.

First buses do not give change as the driver has no access to cash, however all buses also accept payment by contactless card. If paying in hard cash, you put your money in a slot that checks the amount and deposits it in a storage box. An all-day ticket that can be used on any First bus costs £4.50 for the city zone, or £5.50 for the entire First Glasgow network. A weekly ticket costs £16.50 for the inner city or £19.50 for the whole wider network which can take you as far as, for example, Loch Lomond. Some other bus operators, however, give change.

Other bus operators within the city are McGill's and Stagecoach West Scotland which operate services out to the outlying towns in Renfrewshire and Ayrshire respectively: note that the day/weekly passes bought on First buses will not be valid on these, with the exception of SPT Day Tripper and ZoneCards (explained below).

One of the current scourges of Glasgow, however (in the opinion of locals, at least), is the myriad of private bus operators that supposedly "complement" the core services operated by First, McGills and Stagecoach. In reality, many merely duplicate the routes that already exist: the net result has been the city centre being clogged up with empty (and often badly maintained) buses, and for the visitor the key thing to remember is that some of these operators do not accept any of the SPT day passes. On the flip side, they keep the somewhat extortionate prices of First Glasgow in check. The situation is currently a political hot potato among locals.

Unless you don't scare easily, it's best to avoid Glasgow buses heading out of town later than 22:00 on Friday or Saturday nights.

By car

Because of its compact size and extensive public transport system, it is not really necessary to drive around the centre of Glasgow. In fact, for the visitor, driving in the central area can be a stressful and very slow experience thanks to the almost unfathomable one way system (particularly in and around the business district around Blythswood Hill and Anderston), bus lanes (monitored by police cameras) and pedestrianised streets. Coupled with impatient and often aggressive drivers that don't make the best use of available lanes at the frustratingly long duration and frequent traffic lights, it is often better for your blood pressure and average journey times to get out and walk! Despite the distinctive American style grid plan of streets (virtually unique among the UK's large cities), the city *doesn't* have the American street naming system, so visitors from the US and Canada in particular should note talking in the language of "blocks" to a local will only result in confusion.

Fares

Strathclyde Partnership for Transport (SPT) is the local agency which operates the subway and co-ordinates public transport in the Greater Glasgow area. SPT offers a number of different daily combined bus/rail travel tickets aimed at the visitor.

The <u>Mackintosh Trail</u> ticket allows unlimited travel on the subway and First's bus services in Greater Glasgow after 09:30 Monday to Friday and all day on Saturday and Sunday, and costs £10. It also includes entry to all participating Mackintosh attractions in and around Glasgow.

The Roundabout ticket gives complete freedom of the subway and the suburban rail network within the Greater Glasgow area, which includes the city boundary and most of the surrounding towns, for £6.30 after 09:30 Monday to Friday and all day on Saturday and Sunday.

The Day Tripper ticket covers the entire Strathclyde rail network, which extends as far south as Barrhill in South Ayrshire, some 68 mi south of Glasgow, and Ardlui at the northern tip of **Loch Lomond**, some 40 mi north on the West Highland Railway. It has the added advantage of being accepted by the subway, most bus operators in the Strathclyde region and on the Kilcreggan and Renfrew ferries. Two versions are available; for 1 adult and up to 2 children (£11.20) or 2 adults and up to 4 children (£19.80). You can buy it only from a staffed rail station, SPT Travel Centre or online.

If you are in town for a week or more, SPT's ZoneCard might be useful. It can be used on suburban trains, buses, and the underground and is valid all day, even in the morning. Prices vary depending on how long you want it for (1 week to 1 year) and how many zones that you want it to cover.

By taxi

Like most major British cities, you have two options. Your first option is the traditional London-style black cabs which can be hailed from the side of the road (look out for the yellow "Taxi" sign being illuminated). The fleet is operated by Glasgow Taxis, and can also be ordered by telephone (+44 141 429-7070). There are taxi ranks outside Central and Queen Street railway stations, adjacent to George Square and along the southern end of Queen Street itself. There is also a taxi rank located at Buchanan Bus Station. For a journey from say the centre of town to the West End expect to pay around £5-£6, from the city centre out to the suburbs around £10-£12. Be aware that some drivers will refuse to take you outside the city boundary, but some will if you offer a good price for them.

Your second option is by private hire or minicab. Unlike the black cabs, these cannot be hailed, and you must book by telephone. There is a myriad of private hire operators which are cheaper than black cabs: their phone numbers are clearly displayed on the back of the vehicles. Never use unlicensed private taxis, which can sometimes be seen touting for business outside nightclubs near closing time and near legitimate taxi ranks. Always look for the yellow Glasgow City Council licence plate attached to the rear bumper of the vehicle if unsure. Glasgow

Private Hire is one of the biggest taxi fleets in Europe and has thousands of cars, which service all areas of the city. They can be reached on a variety of different numbers (including +44 141 774-3000). Another popular alternative is Hampden Cabs, which services most of the city and surrounding area. Hampden Cabs can be contacted on +44 141 649-5050 (though Irish visitors should be aware they employ a driver who once threw four passengers out of his cab for the 'crime' of speaking Irish).

By boat

There is now a River Bus service, which picks up tourists from central Glasgow (Broomielaw Pontoon) and takes them to, amongst other sites of interest, the Glasgow Science Centre, and the Clydebuilt (Maritime) Museum. There is also a ferry from Yoker on the north bank of the River Clyde to the town of Renfrew on the opposite bank which is within walking distance of Braehead shopping centre and the Xscape leisure complex. The Renfrew Ferry now carries only foot passengers and bicycles. It stopped carrying cars in 1984 after the Clyde Tunnel opened just a few miles upriver. From 1984 to 2010 the Renfrew Ferry carried passengers on two smaller-sized ferries, MV Yoker Swan and MV Renfrew Rose. Clydelink took over operation of the Renfrew Ferry in 2010.

Seeing

Architecture

As befits a city that was at its richest through the 19th century and at the beginning of the 20th, the centre of Glasgow has a fine legacy of Victorian and Edwardian buildings with their lavish interiors and spectacular carved stonework. Outside of the central area the main streets are lined with the legendary tenements - the city's trademark 3 or 4 story residential buildings built from red or blonde sandstone which positively glow during the summer. The controversial *Bruce Report* of the late 1940s triggered a massive regeneration programme which lasted into the late 1970s and saw huge swathes of tenement housing literally wiped out to make way for soulless housing estates and high-rise tower blocks, whilst in the city centre, many large concrete office buildings were built of often questionable architectural merit. The few surviving examples worthy of note for those fans of Brutalist architecture are the massive twin 30-storey Camlachie tower blocks in the East End (sadly scheduled for demolition in 2014), Sir Robert Matthew's Riverside estate in the Gorbals, and the gargantuan Anderston Centre by Sir Richard Seifert, close to the Kingston Bridge. Many of these buildings are now being replaced by modern glass and steel structures -

epitomised by the likes of the Radisson Hotel on Argyle Street and the new BBC Scotland building on Pacific Quay.

Glasgow was also the home of Charles Rennie Mackintosh, one of the "Glasgow Four," a group of leading proponents of art nouveau architecture. Indeed, during his lifetime, Mackintosh was probably better regarded abroad than he was in his native Glasgow, even apparently inspiring Frank Lloyd Wright and was recently resurrected as one of the city's most beloved sons. As well as many fine originals and his *magnum opus*, the Glasgow School of Art, many other knock-offs and impersonations exist. However, despite the 'cult' of Mackintosh, Glasgow produced many other fine architects, the best known of whom is probably Alexander 'Greek' Thomson.

The following list is a selection of significant buildings in Glasgow, roughly arranged starting in the City Centre and moving west and south:

Glasgow Cathedral (Cathedral of Saint Mungo), Cathedral Square, Castle Street, +44 141 552-6891. Summer: M-Sa 9:30AM-5:30PM, Su 1PM-5PM; Winter: 9:30AM-4:30PM, Su 1PM-4:30PM. A fine example of Gothic architecture dating from medieval times and built on a site first consecrated in 397 AD.

Behind the cathedral atop a steep hill is the Necropolis cemetery dominated by the statue of John Knox and described by Victorians as a literal "City of The Dead". Free.

City Chambers, George Square (train: Glasgow Queen Street), +44 141 287-2000. Guided tours M-F at 10:30 & 14:30. This imposing structure in George Square was built in 1888 in the Italian Renaissance style and is the headquarters of Glasgow City Council. Tours of the building are available daily, and visitors can see the magnificent marble staircases, lobbies, see the debating chamber and the lavish banqueting hall. In front the building, George Square, the city's notional centre, is populated by several statues of civic leaders and famous figures from history and is often used for outdoor events. Free.

Glasgow Cross, At the junction of Trongate, Saltmarket, High Street, Gallowgate and London Road. This intersection marks the original medieval centre of the city and is dominated by the clock tower of the original City Chambers (destroyed by fire in 1926), and the small hexagonal building known as the Tolbooth. Just to the west on Trongate is the Tron Theatre, a former church that was turned into a prominent theatre.

St Enoch Subway Station, St Enoch Square, Argyle and Buchanan Streets (subway: St Enoch). Always visible. The original subway station, a quaint building now used as a coffee shop, sits in the middle of St Enoch Square. Free.

Glasgow Central Station, Gordon Street, between Union and Hope Streets (train: Glasgow Central), 08457 11 41 41. M-Sa 04:00-00:30, Su 07:00-00:30. The city's principal railway terminus, which is worth entering for its grand interior, which you can access from Gordon Street on the north side of the building. On the exterior, a feature of note is the massive glass walled bridge (known as Hielanman's Umbrella) which spans Argyle Street and holds up the tracks and platforms. There's also an excellent station tour exploring the hidden corners of the station guided by a Network Rail historian (£10) Free.

Willow Tea Rooms, 217 Sauchiehall St, +44 141 332-0521. During the temperance movement, the idea of "tearooms", places where you could relax and enjoy non-alcoholic refreshments in differently themed rooms, became popular in Glasgow. This one, designed by Charles Rennie Mackintosh in 1904, was the most popular of its time and has been lovingly restored.

Glasgow School of Art, 167 Renfrew St (subway: Cowcaddens), +44 141 353-4526. Tour schedules vary by season. Seen as one of Charles Rennie Mackintosh's finest buildings, housing one of Britain's pre-eminent schools of art, design and architecture. Guided tours of the building are available (you must book in advance), or if you want to create your own art in the building, you can enrol for evening classes or the summer school. £8.75 adults, £7 students/seniors, £4 youth.

Mitchell Library, North Street (train: Charing Cross), +44 141 287-2999. M-Th 09:00-20:00, F-Sa 09:00-17:00, closed Su. One of Glasgow's best public buildings, it is the largest municipal public reference library in Europe. The imposing structure houses a spectacular reading room, although it has to be said much of the Mitchell's extensive collection is housed in the rather ugly 1970s extension attached to the rear. You can easily lose a day in here! Free.

There are a number of interesting bridges over the River Clyde in the City Centre. The Tradeston Pedestrian Bridge crosses the river east of the M8 motorway and is nicknamed the "Squiggly Bridge" by locals because of its distinctive S-shape. Nearby, the Kingston Bridge carries the M8 motorway across the Clyde. Built in 1969, the bridge is far more spectacular to stand beneath than drive over, with an almost cathedral-like vista and a strange aura of calmness that betrays the likely traffic chaos that is going unseen directly above your head. Further west, the Clyde Arc, locally referred to as the "Squinty Bridge", is a relatively new and prominent bridge over the River Clyde that has an elegant curved design and is unique for how it crosses the river at an angle.

Clyde Auditorium, Exhibition Way (train: Exhibition Centre), +44 141 248 3000. Affectionately known by Glaswegians as the Armadillo, this building is a concert hall which forms part of the Scottish Exhibition and Conference Centre complex. Designed by Sir Norman Foster, and contrary to popular belief, *not*inspired by the Sydney Opera House, it is in fact supposed to represent ship's hulls. The auditorium has now garnered some world fame for being the place where the Susan Boyle audition - one of the most downloaded YouTube video clips in history - was filmed.

Glasgow University, University Avenue (subway: Hillhead), +44 141-330 5511. Exterior and campus always visible; Visitor centre M-Sa 9:30AM-5PM. Founded as an institution in 1451, the University itself is the fourth oldest in the entire United Kingdom, and one of the most prestigious academic institutions in the country. Contains the Hunterian Museum and Art Gallery, including a reconstruction of Mackintosh's house. The exterior of the main building is fine in its own right; the current main University building is neo-gothic and dates from 1870, designed by Sir George Gilbert Scott (the man who also designed London's St Pancras railway station). The main building has an interesting visitor's centre (open all year round) which is free and sits atop a drumlin with commanding views over Kelvingrove Park and the western fringes of the city. Free.

Atop a steep hill across Kelvingrove Park from the university is Park Circus, an area of Georgian town houses laid out in a radial pattern similar to the English city of Bath. This neighbourhood has made the transition from originally being an upmarket residential area to a prestigious office district for mainly legal and consultancy firms, although in recent years there have been moves to encourage the companies back into the city centre and return the buildings to residential use. If you make the effort to walk through Kelvingrove Park, go up to this area as it is worth descending down the grand Granite Staircase, on the south side of the hill facing the river.

Scotland Street School, 225 Scotland St (*subway: Shields Road*), +44 141 287 0500. Tu-Th and Sa 10AM–5PM, F and Su 11AM–5PM, closed M. Charles Rennie Mackintosh's last major building - thoughtfully designed, with an excellent museum covering both Mackintosh and the changing faces of schools. Free.

House for an Art Lover, Bellahouston Park (*train: Dumbreck or subway: Ibrox*),+44 141 353 4770. Opening times vary. Built in the 1990s to Mackintosh's original 1901 entry for a design competition. £4.50 adults, £3 youth/students.

Holmwood House, 61-63 Netherlee Rd (*in Cathcart, in the South Side of the city*), 0844 493 2204. Summer months only, Th-M 12PM-5PM. Now run by the National Trust, and currently in the process of being renovated, Holmwood House is one of the best examples of the work of Glasgow's other great architect: Alexander 'Greek' Thomson. £6 adults, £16 family, £5 concession.

If this just whets your appetite for information on Glasgow's architecture, try and get hold of a copy of *Central Glasgow: An Illustrated Architectural Guide*, by Charles McKean and others. There are various ions (ISBN:1873190220, ISBN:1851582002, ISBN:1851582010).

Museums and art galleries

The Victorians also left Glasgow with a wonderful legacy of museums and art galleries, which the city has dutifully built upon. The following list is only a selection. The city council alone runs several museums and galleries. Visitors should be aware that most of the galleries appear to be closed on Sundays, and that - to the understandable annoyance of many visitors to Glasgow - most of the museums shut their doors at 17:00.

Burrell Collection, 2060 Pollokshaws Rd, Pollok Country Park (*train: Pollokshaws West, then walk through Pollok Park*), +44 141 287 2550. M-Th, Sa 10:00-17:00; F/Su 11:00-17:00. This is a collection of over 9,000 artworks gifted to the city of Glasgow by Sir William Burrell and housed in a purpose-built museum in the Pollok Estate in the south of the city. Free.

Gallery of Modern Art, Royal Exchange Square (*on Queen Street in the City Centre*), +44 141 287 3050. M-W, Sa 10:00-17:00, Th 10:00-20:00, F/Su 11:00-17:00. This gallery houses a terrific collection of recent paintings and sculptures, with space for new exhibitions. In the basement is one of Glasgow's many public libraries, with free internet access and cafe. Free.

Glasgow Police Museum, 30 Bell Street, +44 141 552-1818. Summer : M-Sa 10 :00-16 :30, Su 12:00-16:30; Winter: Tu 10:00-16:30, Su 12:00-16:30, closed M and W-Sa. The Glasgow police force is the oldest in Britain, dating back to 1779. It has dealt with a number of famous cases, and many of the paraphernalia relating to some of these are in this museum; there is also a section dealing with the history of police forces throughout the world. Recently opened up in new premises (2010). Free.

Glasgow Science Centre, 50 Pacific Quay (*train: Exhibition Centre or subway: Cessnock*), +44 141 420 5000. Summer: Daily 10AM-5PM; Winter: W-F 10AM-3PM, Sa-Su 10AM-5PM, closed M-Tu. Has hundreds of interactive science exhibits for children, an IMAX cinema, and the 125-meter Glasgow Tower, the only tower in the world which can rotate through 360 degrees from its base. £10 adults, £8 children/seniors; add £2.50 for planetarium or IMAX cinema.

Hunterian Museum and Art Gallery, University of Glasgow, University Avenue, +44 141 330 4221. Tu-Sa 10AM-5PM, Su 11AM-4PM, closed M. The art gallery contains a world famous Whistler collection, and various temporary exhibitions. It also contains The Mackintosh House, a reconstruction of the principal interiors from the Glasgow home of the Scottish architect and designer Charles Rennie Mackintosh (1868-1928). The separate museum is the oldest public museum in Scotland and has a variety of exhibits, including a display on the Romans in Scotland (featuring items found in the Roman Fort in Bearsden), one on the various dinosaur discoveries found on the Isle of Skye, and various temporary exhibitions. Free; Mackintosh House £5 adults, £3 concessions.

Kelvingrove Art Gallery and Museum, Argyle Street (subway: Kelvinhall), +44 141 276 9599. M-Th, Sa 10AM-5PM; F, Su 11AM-5PM. The city's grandest public museum, with one of the finest civic collections in Europe housed within this Glasgow Victorian landmark. The collection is quite varied, with artworks, biological displays and anthropological artifacts. The museum as a whole is well-geared towards children and families, with "discovery center" rooms of interactive exhibits and all the displays labeled with easy-to-understand descriptions. The "Life" wing holds fossils, wildlife displays, artifacts from ancient Egypt, exhibits on the Scottish people, a hall of arms and armor, and even a Supermarine Spitfire hanging in the main hall of the wing. The "Expression" wing holds a fantastic collection of fine and decorative arts, including Salvador Dali's celebrated "Crucifixion of St. John of the Cross" painting and select works by renowned artists like Van Gogh, Monet and Rembrandt, as well as a hall of period Glasgow furnishings by Mackintosh. The main hall has a functioning organ, and daily recitals are played in the afternoon. Free.

Old Govan Church and Govan Stones, 866 Govan Rd (*Subway: Govan*), +44 141 440-2466 (). Summer: check website; Winter: by appointment. Discover the unique collection of early medieval stones carved in the 9th to 11th centuries to commemorate the power of those who ruled the Kingdom of Strathclyde. One of Glasgow's most important historical and cultural assets, explore the 31 monuments within the beautiful setting of Govan Old Church. Free.

People's Palace and Winter Gardens, Glasgow Green, +44 141 276 0788. People's Palace Tu-Th, Sa 10AM–5PM, F, Su 11AM–5PM, closed M; Winter Gardens Daily 10AM-5PM. The People's Palace is a great folk museum, telling the history of Glasgow and its people, from various perspectives, displaying details of Glasgow life (including one of Billy Connolly's banana boots). The Winter Gardens, adjacent, is a pleasant greenhouse with a reasonable cafe. Free.

Provand's Lordship, 3 Castle Street (opposite *Glasgow Cathedral*), +44 141 276 1625. Tu-Th, Sa 10AM-5PM; F, Su 11AM-5PM, closed M. Glasgow's oldest remaining house, built in 1471, has been renovated to give visitors and idea what the inside of a Glasgow house was like circa 1700.Free.

Riverside Museum, 100 Pointhouse Place (*subway: Kelvinhall*), +44 141 287 2720. M-Th and Sa 10AM-5PM, F and Su 11AM-5PM. A recently reopened museum with an excellent collection of vehicles and models to tell the story of transport by land and sea, with a unique Glasgow flavour. Besides the usual rail locomotives, buses, trams, cars and planes, the museum also includes a recreated subway station and a street scene of old Glasgow. Behind the museum is the Tall Ship, the Glenlee, built in 1896 and one of only five Clydebuilt sailing ships that remain afloat in the world today, now restored and open to the public. Free; Tall Ship £5 adults, £3 children (first child free with paying adult).

Sharmanka, Trongate 103, +44 141 552 7080. Performances Th and Su 7PM or by individual appointment. A kinetic gallery / theatre. It consists of a number of strange machines created by the Russian artists Eduard Bersudsky. The machines perform stories and the light and sound during the performance adds to a really unique and amazing experience. £8, £5 concessions, children under 16 free.

St. Mungo's Museum of Religious Life and Art, 2 Castle Street (*next to the Glasgow Cathedral*), +44 141 276 1625. Tu-Th, Sa 10AM-5PM, F, Su 11AM-5PM, closed M. This museum features exhibits relating not only to Glasgow's patron saint and the growth of Christianity in the city, but numerous exhibits pertaining to many faiths practised locally and worldwide. Free.

Street Level Photoworks, Trongate 103, +44 141 552 2151. Tu-Sa 10AM-5PM, Su 12PM-5PM, closed M. An alternative art gallery/installation space. Free.

Tenement House, 145 Buccleuch Street, 0844 493 2197. Summer months only, Daily 1PM-5PM. A National Trust for Scotland site, a middle class Glasgow tenement house preserved in pretty much the way it was in the early 20th century. £6 adults, £16 family, £5 concessions.

Transmission Gallery, 28 King Street, +44 141 552 7141. Tu-W, F-Sa 11AM-5PM, Th 11AM-8PM. A gallery set up in 1983 by ex-students of the Glasgow School of Art as a hub for the local art community and to provide exhibition space. Free.

Parks

For a large city, Glasgow has a surprising number of parks and green spaces; there is more parkland here than in any other British city.

Bellahouston Park.

Botanic Gardens. A major park in the West End (the most popular aside from Kelvingrove), the Botanic Gardens contains extensive tropical and temperate plant collections from around the world.

Glasgow Green, (*train: Bridgeton or Argyle Street, then walk or take the bus along London Road*). The most famous of the Glasgow parks, Glasgow Green was founded by Royal grant in 1450 and has slowly been enclosed by the city and evolved from grazing land into a modern public park. "The Green" as its known to the locals is one of the major venues for concerts and open air events in Glasgow. Among the highlights are the People's Palace and Winter Gardens (covered above), Nelson's Memorial, an obelisk or needle: built to commemorate Nelson's victory at the battle of Trafalgar, the Templeton Carpet Factory, with its ornate brick work (now a business center), and the Doulton Fountain, the largest terracotta fountain in the world. There is limited official parking in or around the green and the area is notorious for car crime. Be aware the council will tow away illegally parked vehicles and charge you up to £250 pounds to get them back!

<u>Kelvingrove Park</u>. In the city's West End, this is also a very popular park, particularly with the students from the nearby University. The most prominent landmark here is the Kelvingrove Art Gallery and Museum (covered above) on the banks of the River Kelvin which runs through the park. It also contains a recently constructed skate park.

<u>Mugdock Park</u>.

<u>Queen's Park</u>.

<u>Strathclyde Country Park</u>.

<u>Victoria Park</u>.

<u>Fossil Grove</u>, Victoria Park, +44 141 276 1695. Summer months only; Daily 10AM-4PM. The remains of an ancient forest, around 330 million years old. This is the only example of a preserved forest from this period on Earth.

Tollcross Park, 254B Wellshot Rd G32 7AX. Tollcross Park is internationally famous for its unique Rose Garden and impressive Winter Gardens. The park has many hidden gems including the Glen Nature Walk, Children's Farm and Courtyard Visitor Centre. The park is full of points of interest and offers a welcome retreat from the busy surrounding streets. The park is open from dawn until dusk. However, the specific facilities in the park may differ. Free.

Doing

There are many nightclubs, concerts and festivals in Glasgow.

Music

Glasgow's been famous for its music scene(s) for at least 20 years, with some top acts literally queuing to play at venues such as the Barrowlands or King' Tuts. There's plenty of venues where you're likely to see a good band (and lots of bad bands too); on any day of the week there should be at least several shows to choose from throughout the city, with the number increasing to a even greater variety on Thursday, Friday & Saturday. In no particular order, here follows some pop/indie/rock-orientated venues:

<u>Nice 'n' Sleazy</u> on Sauchiehall St. Open til 3AM every night of the week, with bands on practically every night also. Gigs are downstairs and bar upstairs plays a variety of alternative/rock/punk. Over 18's only (both bar and gigs) .

<u>The Barrowland Ballroom</u> (*Gallowgate, 0.5km from Glasgow Cross*) The Barrowlands, as it is commonly known, is arguably the city's most famous and most respected live venue - famous for its sprung floor and excellent acoustics

<u>King Tut's Wah Wah Hut</u> on St Vincent St, where both Oasis and, local favourites, Glasvegas were discovered. <u>ABC</u> on Sauchiehall St.

<u>13th Note</u> on King St (just off Argyle Street/Trongate). nMaggie <u>May's</u> (*Merchant City, on the corner of Trongate and Albion Street*) Pub/restaurant with a lively programme of up and coming bands. <u>The Cathouse</u> on Union St (close to the junction with Argyle Street).

<u>The Riverside Club</u> (33 Fox Street - behind St Enoch Square) Glasgow's top ceilidh (Scottish country dancing) venue on Friday and Saturday nights.

<u>Mono</u> restaurant and record shop. <u>Stereo</u> City centre venue with regular indie gigs downstairs, bar and cafe upstairs. <u>Glasgow O2 Academy</u> on Eglinton St (*nearest Subway: Bridge Street*). <u>The Arches</u> on Argyle St (underneath *the "Hielanman's Umbrella" of Central Station*). Running one of the UK's best techno nights; Pressure. Recently celebrated 10 year anniversary. Note: this is also a theatrical and arts venue, a pub and restaurant.

<u>Sub Club</u> on Jamaica St (*nearest rail: Central Station*). Recently celebrated 20 years, rated one of the best clubs in the world from house to techno to whatever takes your fancy.

<u>The Tunnel</u> on Mitchell Street: with the Sub Club and the Arches one of Glasgow's premier dance clubs: frequently hosts top DJ's from round the world, although doesn't quite have The Arches' or the Sub Club's 'underground' reputation. <u>The Vale</u> on Dundas St (adjacent to Buchanan Street subway/Queen Street railway station).

<u>QMU</u> at University Gardens (West End; nearest Subway: Hillhead). <u>The Classic Grand</u> on Union Street/Jamaica Street (*adjacent to Central Station*), a former adult cinema now re-purposed as an alternative music venue. Serves the

rock/metal/punk/alternative scene 4 nights a week with drinks as low as £1.

The Scottish Exhibition & Conference Centre (*rail: Exhibition Centre*) is the city's premier music venue for major headline acts, even if the acoustics of the halls have always been questionable. More intimate gigs are held in the neighbouring Clyde Auditorium (or Armadillo). SECC Tickets sells tickets for these.

Arts and Theatrical Venues

The Glasgow Royal Concert Hall, Sauchiehall Street (*nearest Subway: Buchanan Street*). This is the home of The Royal Scottish National Orchestra, one of Europe's leading symphony orchestras. It also produces the world famous Celtic Connections Festival every January.

The Royal Scottish Academy of Music and Drama (RSAMD), 100 Renfrew Street, is primarily a teaching college but also puts on theatrical and musical performances. It puts on mainly contemporary music, modern dance and jazz. The Theatre Royal, 282 Hope Street, was first opened in 1867. It puts on mainly 'serious' theatre, opera and ballet.

The Tron, 63 Trongate, specialises in contemporary works. St Andrews in the Square, St Andrew's Square, a restored 18th century church turned Arts venue. It puts on classical music and folk.

The Citizens Theatre, 119 Gorbals Street, is one of the most famous theatres in the world, and has launched the careers of many international movie and theatre stars. It specialises in contemporary and avant-garde work.

The King's Theatre, 297 Bath Street, is Glasgow's major 'traditional' theatre. It is over 100 years old, and in the midst of a major refurbishment. The Pavilion, 121 Renfield Street, is the only privately run theatre in Scotland. It was founded in 1904 and has seen many of the greatest stars of music hall perform there: most famously Charlie Chaplin. Nowadays it features mainly 'popular' theatre, musicals and comedy.

The Panopticon Music Hall, off Argyle Street, Trongate, is the oldest surviving music hall in the world (it opened in 1857). It most famously held the debut performance of Stan Laurel (of Laurel and Hardy fame) in 1906. It now shows mainly music hall orientated shows: e.g. magic, burlesque and comedy, but also occasionally puts on classical and world music.

<u>Oran Mor</u> 731 Great Western Road. Restaurant, pub, nightclub, theatrical and music venue. Due to its late opening hours, this venue now lies at the heart of the West End social scene.

The <u>Glasgow International Jazz Festival</u> is held every year in June. Other arts or music festivals of note include <u>The West End Festival</u>, the <u>Merchant City Festival</u> and numerous others. As always, consult the listings magazine <u>The List</u> for further details.

Comedy

There are two main venues for stand-up comedy in Glasgow.

➢ <u>The Stand</u> on Woodlands Road (West End)

➢ <u>Jongleurs</u> in the City Centre

Although other pubs and clubs frequently hold comedy events: see the listings magazine The List for details.

CF also the Magners Glasgow International Comedy Festival held yearly thoroughout March/April.

Cinema

The most interesting films in Glasgow are shown at:

➢ <u>Glasgow Film Theatre</u> (GFT), 12 Rose St, 332 8128. Excellent choice of classics, also art and foreign-language movies.

➢ <u>The Grosvenor</u>, Ashton Lane (just off Byres Road in the West End).

➢ <u>CCA</u>, on Sauchiehall St. Shows films, though it's primarily an art gallery.

Mainstream films can be seen at the *Cineworld* on Renfrew St, which is the tallest cinema in the world

Football

Glasgow also has the 3 biggest football stadia in Scotland. The major events in the football season are the clashes between the two major clubs; Celtic and Rangers. Known as the "Old Firm", with their sectarian undertones, these 90 minute matches produce a profound effect on the city, occasionally, but less frequently in recent times; resulting in violent clashes during or after the game. The Old Firm Derby is generally considered to be one of the best derby matches in the world, in terms of passion and atmosphere generated by both sets of fans, and is considered by many neutrals to be the most intense rivalry in all of Britain.

The match itself is always highly anticipated and much talked about before and after. Cup (non-league) ties between these two giants are quite frequent, raising the tensions further. Be aware that getting tickets for "Old Firm" games can be difficult and cup ties near impossible. Following Rangers' well publicised liquidation in 2012 and its subsequent demotion to the lower leagues, it looks likely that an Old Firm derby match at the highest level will now be some years off - this may a blessing or a disappointment depending on your point of view! If you do go to one of these matches it is advised that you do not wear team colours (blue/red/white for Rangers, green/white for Celtic) after the match.

Hampden Park (Home of Football) (Nearest Rail: Mount Florida - depart from Glasgow Central) Scotland's national stadium , capacity 52,063. Hampden hosts many large sporting events and concerts and also houses the Scottish Football Museum. The Scottish national football team plays its home games here. Is also home to Queen's Park Football Club. It is probably most famous for hosting the 1960 European Cup Final between Real Madrid and Eintracht Frankfurt. In more recent times, the UEFA Champion's League Final was held in 2002 between Real Madrid and Bayer Leverkusen and the UEFA Cup Final in 2007 between Seville and Espanyol. It is possible for visitors to have a tour of the Stadium and the Scottish Football Museum..

Celtic Park (Kerrydale Street, Parkhead - First Bus 40/61/62/240/262 go past the stadium) Home of Celtic Football Club, which has a capacity of 60,832 - making it the biggest "club" stadium in Scotland and the second largest in the UK, behind only Manchester United's Old Trafford ground. By visiting the Celtic Visitors' Centre, you can take a guided tour of the stadium as well as taking a trip through the history of the club through our various informative and impressive exhibitions and auditorium. To experience Celtic take one of our guided tours available from Monday to Sunday 11am, 12 noon, 1.45pm and 2.30pm (except home matchdays). Saturday Matchday tours available at 9.30, 10.00, 10.30 and 11.00. Adults £8.50, Concessions £5.50 Family Ticket £20 (2 adults and 2 children or 1 adult and 3 children) Under 5's are admitted free.

Ibrox Stadium, (Subway: Ibrox) This is the home of Rangers Football Club , capacity 51,082. Ibrox tours run every Friday, Saturday and Sunday (non match days only!)) and are priced at just £5.50 for kids, £8 for adults and £24.50 for a family group (2 adults and 2 children). On the Ibrox tour, you will get exclusive access to the home dressing room and hear a recorded message from Walter Smith and Ally McCoist. Climb the marble staircase, visit the illustrious Trophy Room, the Blue Room and Manager's

Office. Take a virtual tour of the Club's state of the art training facility at Murray Park and even run down the tunnel before taking the Manager's seat in the dugout! Tickets, except for matches against Celtic, are easily available online from the club's website, ticket centre at the stadium and club outlets at JJB Sports Stores in Glasgow city centre.

Club merchandise is available from the JJB Rangers Megastore located at the stadium and JJB Sports stores in Glasgow, with unofficial merchandise readily available in the environs of the stadium on matchdays. Food is available at the stadium in the Argyll House restaurant and the various burger stands in and around the stadium concourses. The Sportsmans Chip Shop on the Copland Road adjacent to the Stadium is also popular with the supporters. There are various bars beside the stadium, the Louden Tavern on the Copland Road being the closest. Along the Paisley Road West are numerous bars sympathetic to the Rangers cause, such as the Louden Tavern, the Grapes Bar, District Bar and the Kensignton Bar to name but a few.

Firhill, - Home of Partick Thistle Football Club, also known as "the Jags" (and not actually in the suburb of Partick - the club is actually located in Maryhill). It has a capacity of 10,887. Partick

Thistle matches are a good way to see the Glaswegian passion for 'fitba' (football) without the unpleasantness of the Old Firm rivalry, or the high prices for their games.

Other Sport

- ➢ Braehead Clan, - Increasingly popular ice hockey, with an Americanised, family, razzmatazz feels.

- ➢ Glasgow Rocks, - Basketball team who play home games at the Emirates Arena, directly opposite Celtic Park.

- ➢ Glasgow Warriors, - Rugby team, playing in the Pro12 and the European Professional Club Rugby format.

- ➢ West of Scotland Cricket Club, - Scene of the world's very first international football match, between Scotland and England in 1872, now home of West of Scotland Cricket Club. Licensed bar, friendly atmosphere, regular fixtures in the summer.

Learning and Working

Glasgow has three universities:
University of Glasgow. Located in the west end of the city, this university has served Glasgow since 1451 and is the fourth oldest

in the United Kingdom, and also one of the country's most prestigious.

University of Strathclyde is situated in the north-east of the city centre and was originally founded in 1796 as Anderson's University, and later became the Royal College of Science and Technology (affectionately nicknamed "The Tech" by Glaswegians) before finally gaining full University status in 1964. In 1993 it absorbed the former Jordanhill College of Education, and gained that institution's campus in the West End.

Glasgow Caledonian University, to the north of the city centre, is Glasgow's newest university. It was formed from the merger of Glasgow College of Technology and Queens' College in 1992. Literally a couple of minutes away from Buchanan Bus Station.

Work

Jobs in Glasgow can be found through the government-run JobCentres. Be aware that you will need a National Insurance number and, if you are not a citizen of the European Economic Area or Switzerland, the correct type of work visa to work legally in the UK. Your employer should require this to ensure you pay the correct rates of income tax. However if you ask around you'll find a lot of bars and nightclubs offer work cash-in-hand. Some of the many temp agencies in the city centre aren't too fussy about immigration niceties either. With the city's growing financial services industry, there are quite a lot of opportunities for office temps, though this has changed with the global economic downturn of the last few years.

Buying

Glasgow has positioned itself as an upmarket retail destination, the shopping is the some of the best in Scotland, and generally accepted as the No.2 shopping experience in Britain after London. Buchanan Street is the 7th most expensive place for retail space in the world, which means that there's an increasing number of designer clothes shops in areas like the Merchant City. Alongside this, the Council is putting pressure on more traditional shopping centres like the Barras where you can get remarkably similar-looking clothes for a more sensible price.

The nucleus of Glasgow shopping is the so-called "Golden Z", made up of the continuous pedestrianised thoroughfares of Argyle Street, Buchanan Street and Sauchiehall Street. Here, virtually all of the major British big name retailers are represented. Buchanan Street is the most upmarket of the three, with prestigious names such as House of Fraser, Apple Store and Zara and other specialised designer stores. Ingram Street in the Merchant City has seen a boom in recent years for attracting more exclusive, premium brands like Bose, Bang and Olufsen, Ralph Lauren and so on.

Bath Street and Hope Street run parallel to the main pedestrianised streets, and if you want to get away from "chain store hell", they have a fine selection of more quirky, local independent retailers selling everything from fine art, Scottish clothing, antiques and specialist hi-fi.

There are larger shopping malls on the city outskirts at Braehead, Silverburn and Glasgow Fort.

The Barras in the East End is the essential Glasgow shopping experience. Hundreds of market stalls selling everything you could possibly want and a load of other stuff too. Free entertainment available from time to time when the Police raid the place for counterfeit goods. All year Sa-Su 10:00-17:00; weekday opening in the weeks immediately before Christmas. This market is notorious for counterfeit good; especially DVDs and clothing. Pirated DVDs should be avoided at all costs, as the quality is often very poor.

The <u>Buchanan Galleries</u> , Buchanan Street, is a large shopping mall in the heart of the city centre which has all the usual British high street stores, its anchor tenant is John Lewis.

The <u>St Enoch Centre</u> . Europe's largest glass roofed building - this huge mall is on St Enoch Square between Argyle Street and Buchanan Street, and a major extension and refurbishment programme was completed in 2010.

<u>Princes Square</u> is an upmarket mall just off Buchanan Street in the city centre. Specialises in designer clothes shops, jewellery and audio equipment. Note, Grande Dame of British Fashion Vivienne Westwood has a store as well as a separate jewellery concession in Princes Square.

The <u>Argyle Arcade</u> is the city's jewellery quarter housing Scotland's largest collection of jewellery shops. The L-shaped arcade connects Argyle Street and Buchanan Street. Shops here vary considerably - there are a selection of cheaper jewellery shops and a selection of luxury prestigious jewellers. Very commonly used as a short cut for shoppers between Buchanan Street and Argyle Street.

De Courcy's Arcade is an unusual little shopping arcade with lots of second hand music and book shops and independent gift shops. Located just off Byres Road in the west end (*subway: Hillhead*)

Byres Road. Check out the chichi shops and vintage stores in the West End

Fat Buddha Store, 73 St Vincent Street, +44 141 226 8972. 9.30-6pm. Fat Buddha has become an institution in Glasgow since it opened its doors back in 2006, the only streetwear store in the city, it also stocks a wide range of books, magazines, homewares and carried the over 400 colours of spray paint, featured in the New York Times and appears in the Taschen Book 48 hours in Europe. Open every day, offering free Wi-Fi and coffee in the Book section, its a great place to whittle away a few hours. mid.

Eating

The city has won the title "Curry Capital of Britain" two years running and has a huge and dynamic range of restaurants, Indian or otherwise. Despite Glasgow being the home town of culinary hero Gordon Ramsay, there are no Michelin-starred fine dining establishments in the city (Glasgow's sole Michelin starred restaurant, *Amaryllis* - owned by Ramsay himself - embarrassingly folded in 2004), nevertheless there are scores of highly regarded eateries in the city. The restaurants below are some of the culinary highlights of Glasgow.

Scottish/Local

The Ubiquitous Chip (*12 Ashton Lane, West End; Subway - Hillhead*). Of all Ashton Lane's establishments, "The Chip" as it is popularly known by locals is certainly its most celebrated and most famous. Established by the late great Ronnie Clydesdale - a local legend - this local restaurant has been serving up top quality food using Scottish produce since the early 1970s and is frequently lauded as one of Scotland's finest restaurants. On the expensive side, but well worth it. Booking absolutely essential.

Arisaig, (*1 Merchant Square, Candleriggs - Merchant City, nearest railway: Queen Street*). Another celebrated Glasgow eatery, bar and brasserie notable for its extensive list of wines and Scottish malt whiskies. Also has music nights.

Bart&Urby's, 145 Vincent St, Local pub food, beers and ales. American diner style. The Red Onion, (*247 West Campbell Street, nearest railway - Central/Charing Cross*). Perched high up on Blythswood Hill, this locally owned restaurant uses local produce within international dishes produced by recognised chef John Quigley.

The Grill Room at The Square (*29 Royal Exchange Square, - nearest railway: Queen Street*), just along from Roganos, this classy establishment has made a name for itself under the leadership of chef David Friel. Quite pricey but worth it.

The Chardon D'Or, (*176 West Regent Street, Glasgow, G2 4RL*) Owner and head chef Brian Maule is a former business partner of local hero Gordon Ramsay. When Ramsay began his TV career as a celebrity chef, Maule took the chance to branch out on his own and is now a very highly regarded local institution. The result is Chardon D'Or, opened in 2001 and widely recognised as one of the very best quality restaurants in Glasgow. Owner Brian Maule is also well known for strong links with musicians and entertainers, and his restaurant often offers deals combining concerts or shows with fine dining for one fixed price. A popular choice with local businessmen.

Cafe Gandolfi, (*64 Albion Street*). A real Glasgow institution, serving fine locally sourced food in a relaxed and relaxing atmosphere. Great food and great service make this Cafe a must-visit on any trip to Glasgow.

Takeaway/Fish & Chips

Glasgow has taken many different cultural foods and combined them into a unique dining experience. Most takeaways offer Indian dishes (pakora), pizzas and kebabs as well as the more traditional fish and chips or burgers. This has resulted in some takeaways offering a blend of dishes like chips with curry sauce, the donner kebab pizza, the battered and deep fried pizza to name but a few.

Fish & Chips (aka "Fish Supper") is a perennial favourite, and there are a healthy number of fish and chip shops around the city. As mentioned above, many will also offer Asian or Italian dishes alongside the traditional chip shop fayre. Given the Glaswegian's famous fondness for anything deep fried - "bad" establishments don't usually last long. In the centre of town, four of the best "chippies" are:

➢ Jack McPhees, (*City Centre - Hope Street, near Theatre Royal, West End - Byres Road*). Chain of sit down restaurant with table service. Slightly more expensive than a takeaway, but excellent quality.

➢ The Coronation, (*Gallowgate, just beyond Glasgow Cross under the City Union railway bridge*). A Glasgow institution sitting at the gateway into the Barrowlands area - the usual friendly Glaswegian reception and competitively priced.

➢ Da Vinci's, (*City Centre* - Queen *Street*). 24 hour dining in this handily positioned sit-down takeaway near many of the city's nightclubs.

On a side note, the now infamous deep fried Mars Bar - served up in many Glasgow chip shops - did *not* originate in the city, contrary to popular belief. It was in fact invented in Stonehaven in Aberdeenshire.

Chinese

➢ Oriental Yummy, 96 Queen Margaret Drive. - arguably one of the finest Chinese takeaway in the West End with a proud record and loyal following. Home Delivery Fri-Sat: 5pm-11pm (Sun-Thurs til 10pm- CLOSED TUESDAYS). Order Online to save,(OY2 - £2 off next online order).

➢ The Ho Wong, 82 York St. Close to Central Station. Excellent Chinese Restaurant.

➢ Dragon-I, 311-313 Hope St. In the Theatre District. 'Hitlisted' in The List (2008).

➢ Amber Regent, 50 West Regent Street. Equidistant between Queen Street and Central Station.

> China Sea Restaurant, 12 Renfield Street. Right in the heart of Glasgow City Centre, within 1 minute's walking distance from Glasgow Central Station.

> Panda House Menu and prices , *665 Pollokshaws Road,* - arguably one of the finest Chinese takeaway in the South Side with a proud record and loyal following. Home Delivery daily 17:00-23:59. Order Online to save £2 off next online order).

European

Brel, Ashton Lane, Glasgow G12 8SJ (*In the West End off Byres Road - nearest Subway: Hillhead*), Tel. +44 141 342 4966. M-Su 12PM-Late. Located in the dynamic Ashton Lane in the West End of Glasgow, this restaurant is well known for its Belgian fare particularly their Moules (*Mussel*) Pots in a variety of flavours. This Bar/Restaurant is set over 3 levels and sells a range of Belgian beers, including Banana and Raspberry, along with a few of the local Scottish favourites. During the warmer weather there is a large Beer Garden at the rear. There is often free live entertainment. Prices: à la carte menu, starters: £2.95-£4.95 and mains: £8.95-£15.50. Also great deals at *Food Happy Hour* M-Su 5PM-7PM!

<u>Stravaigin</u>, (*28 Gibson Street, West End - nearest Subway: Kelvinbridge*), Tel. +44 141 334 2665, Established by Ronnie Clydesdale (of Ubiquitous Chip fame), and located adjacent to Glasgow University and Kelvingrove Park, this award winning gastro-pub offers a wide selection of both European and World cuisine made from Scottish ingredients. Also renowned for its creative cocktails.

<u>Sloans</u>, Argyle Arcade (*Morrison Court; off Buchanan St or Argyle Street*). Boasts to be 'the oldest bar and restaurant in Glasgow'. You can sit outside if you wish, or try the bistro or other menus. They offer other activities, such as a cinema-EAT experience, ceilidh dancing and more recently various music nights in the upstairs ballroom.

Indian

Glasgow has, arguably, the finest Indian food in the United Kingdom, and indeed many Glaswegians now joke that the Indian Curry is their "national dish". Historically, the city's finest Indian restaurants have been clustered together in the Charing Cross area, just beyond the "main" section of Sauchiehall Street, but in recent years the Merchant City has seen a boom in new establishments. Take your pick from Panjea, The Wee Curry

Shop, Mother India's Cafe and more. Check out the Ashoka West End (1284 Argyle Street, near Kelvingrove), the Ashoka at Ashton Lane or Kama Sutra (Sauchiehall Street) - all of which are owned by the local Ashoka chain. Glasgow's top Indian restaurants include:

- Balti Club: Menu and prices , 66 Woodlands Road, - arguably one of the finest Indian takeaway in the West End with a proud record and loyal following. Home Delivery 7 Days til Midnight and 4am on Fri-Sat. Order Online to save,(code BC2* - top get £2 off when ordering online).

- Mister Singh's India: (149 Elderslie Street, Charing Cross - nearest railway: Charing Cross) The flagship branch of the Ashoka/Harlequin chain and is notable for its waiting staff who wear kilts. Booking is advisable Thursday-Sunday evenings.

- The Shish Mahal: (66-68 Park Road, West End; nearest Subway: Kelvinbridge) Affectionately known simply as "The Shish" by its regulars, this family run establishment has been here for over 50 years.

➢ The Dhabba: (44 Candleriggs, Merchant City) Authentic North Indian restaurant located in the Merchant City and has won numerous awards.

➢ The Dakhin (89 Candleriggs, Merchant City - above the City Merchant) Sister restaurant to The Dhabba, about 50 yards further north on the same street, but this time specialising in South Indian cuisine it has some great pre-theatre deals and is lauded as much as its sibling.

➢ Cafe India: (29 Albion Street, Merchant City) The original Cafe India in Charing Cross was a Glasgow institution before it was burned down in 2006. Now reborn in the Merchant City area, it's re-established itself as one of the city's top curry spots.

➢ Killermont Polo Club: (2022 Maryhill Road; nearest railway: Maryhill). Upmarket Indian restaurant on the main route out to the affluent north western suburbs of the city. Set in a clubhouse setting, it has won numerous awards and accolades.

➢ Chillies West End: , 176-182 Woodlands Road, West End. In a fantastic location just outside the city centre, but not quite in to the west end. Offers a unique way to sample many Indian dishes with a tapas style menu.

There are also literally hundreds of takeaway Indian restaurants around the city on nearly every main street, although the quality of these can be very variable. Some are excellent - comparable with anything you'd find in the city centre, whilst others can be rather poor. To be on the safe side, only go on local recommendation.

Italian

➢ Esca: near the Tron Theatre is good and inexpensive but often busy.

➢ Sofias: (337 Byres Road) Formerly Antipasti. Excellent quality restaurant; does not offer table bookings -- just show up and ask for a table. You won't be waiting long.

➢ Di Maggio's: (Royal Exchange Square, Merchant City; West Nile Street, City Centre) Locally owned chain of family-friendly Italian restaurants with several outlets in the city and outlying towns. Good value and usually no need to book.

- Dino's: (35-41 Sauchiehall Street, immediately opposite Cineworld and Royal Concert Hall) One of Glasgow's oldest and best known Italian restaurants. Good quality and friendly service.

- L'Ariosto: , 92-94 Mitchell Street, Glasgow G1 3NQ (3 minute walk from Central railway station). One of Glasgow's top Italian restaurants - expensive but award winning and offers its own courtyard and live music.

- Jamie's Italian: , 1 George Square (Adjacent to the City Chambers, nearest rail: Glasgow Queen Street) Glasgow branch of the Jamie Oliver empire, although there is little chance of seeing the man himself. No bookings policy, but there have been stories of people being turned away due to overly casual dress.

- La Parmigiana: (447 Great Western Road). One of the best of the West End's Italian restaurants, but more upmarket than most.

- Amarone: (2 Nelson Mandela Place, Glasgow +44 141 333 1122) Stylish restaurant with excellent menu. Highly rated. Mains £8-20.

- Little Italy: (205 Byres Road). More of a cafe than a restaurant, the pizzas, coffee and hot chocolate are phenomenal. Authentic Italian feel to it. A great place for lunch or an informal dinner, or a pizza after a night out in Ashton Lane. A must if you are in the west end of Glasgow.

- Il Pavone Restaurant: Courtyard, Princes Square, 48 Buchanan Street. is regarded as one of the most established, hospitable and fashionable Italian restaurants in Glasgow (within 2 minutes walking distance from Glasgow Central Station).

- Zizzi: have two restaurants: 2nd Floor, Princes Square, 48 Buchanan Street in the city centre , and 8 Cresswell Lane in the West End

Mexican

Pancho Villas: 26 Bell Street, Glasgow G1 1LG (*in the Merchant City area opposite Merchant Square*), Tel. +44 141 552 7737. M-Sa 12PM to Late, Su 5PM - Late. It is often very busy of an evening especially towards the end of the week, so it is best to make a reservation. Prices: Set Meals are available Mo-Th between 12PM-5PM for 2 Courses - £6.95 and 3 Courses - £8.50. A-la-carte Menu, Starters: £2.50-£7.95 and Mains: £8.50-£12.95.

Fish

As befits a port town, Glasgow excels at seafood and fish.

Gamba (225a West George Street), Winner of The List's (local listing magazine) 'Best Restaurant in Glasgow' award, 2003 and 2004. Two AA rosettes.

Mussel Inn (157 Hope Street), Good quality fish restaurant: has a sister restaurant in Edinburgh.

Rogano (11 Exchange Place), Sumptuous 1930s style architecture for a total dining experience. Rogano is a Glasgow institution, but beware, especially if you get sucked into their vintage wine list, this place can be extremely expensive.

Patisseries

Patisserie Valerie, (19 West Nile St, on corner of Drury Street), The legendary London patisserie has now stretched its tentacles far from its native Soho, and is now expanding nationally. Its fans nickname it as "Pat Val's", and the range of fine cakes and gateaux is legendary. Both your bank balance and your waistline will suffer if you get too indulgent!! There is a smaller branch within Central Station

Veggie

For fab veggie food try:

- ➤ The Fast Food Shop: pakora place on Woodlands Road is ideal for guilt-free snacking on the way home from the pub.

- ➤ 13th Note: on King Street. Looks like an anarchist squat when you walk in, and has a full bar, and serves very good veggie (mainly vegan) food. Try the vegan haggis, neeps and tatties, served with a pink-peppercorn cream sauce. Also worth trying are the risotto balls.

- ➤ Mono: over the road in King's Court, is run by the people who established the Note. It has a lighter, airier feel but with an exclusively vegan menu, beers prepared on-site and two shops (food and records).

- ➤ Stereo: vegan pub in the Renfield Lane near the central station.

- ➤ The 78: organic/vegan pub & restaurant in Kelvinhaugh Street (off the west end of Argyle St).

- ➤ Tchai Ovna: tea houses with veggie food, located in West End (off Otago St) and Shawlands.

International

Glasgow is a city of immigrants and has a thriving international food scene.

> ➢ Khublai Khan's: A unique Mongolian Barbecue restaurant that allows you to create your own stir-fry dishes over and over while sampling meat from around the globe.

Also try Mzouda (Moroccan), Cafe Argan (Moroccan), Shallal (Lebanese), Kokuryo (Korean), Koshkemeer (Kurdish), Café Serghei, Konaki(Greek), Alla Turca (Turkish), La Tasca (Spanish), Ichiban (Japanese) and the numerous Thai, and Malaysian and Chinese restaurants.

Drinking

Pubs are arguably the meeting rooms of Scotland's largest city, and many a lively discussion can be heard in a Glasgow bar. There is nothing Glaswegians love more than "putting the world right" over a pint (or three), whether it's the Old Firm, religion, weather, politics or how this year's holidays went. You are guaranteed a warm welcome from the locals, who will soon strike up a conversation.

There are three (or arguably, four) basic drinking areas: these are also good for restaurants. First, there is the West End (the area around Byres Road and Ashton Lane), second there is the stretch of Sauchiehall Street between the end of the pedestrianised area (near Queen Street Station) and Charing Cross (and the various streets off this area). Thirdly there is the Merchant City, which is near Strathclyde University's campus. This is the most 'upmarket' area to drink and eat in, although it still has numerous student dives: start at the University of Strathclyde and wander down towards the Trongate (the West part of this part of town is the gay area).

Staying in the city centre, there are also several hidden gems in and around the Blythswood Square area and the streets between Hope Street and Charing Cross: this being the city's office district however it can feel quite deserted on evenings and weekends. Finally, and up and coming, is the South Side (i.e. South of the Clyde). This used to be very much 'behind the times' socially speaking, but the relocation of the BBC to the South Side and the whole area generally moving 'upmarket' has improved things greatly. Try the area round Shawlands Cross for restaurants, bars, and The Shed nightclub.

Be warned though about dress codes, particularly in some of the more upmarket establishments in the city centre and West End:

sportswear and trainers (sneakers) are often banned, and some door staff are notoriously "selective" about who is allowed in, with arcane "sorry, regulars only mate" entry policies which they will never explain. If confronted with this, take your custom elsewhere. The general "boozer" type pubs have no dress codes, but football shirts (regardless of team) are almost universally banned in all: particularly on weekends. One rule to be aware of is that some clubs and upmarket pubs enforce an unwritten policy of not allowing all-male groups of more than about four people. For this reason, it may be advisable to split into groups of two or three. Some pubs in Glasgow are also exclusively the haunt of Old Firm football fans: again, these will be very crowded on football days, can get very rowdy, and should be avoided. Fortunately they are easy to spot; for example, a large cluster of Celtic-oriented pubs exist in the Barrowlands area, while one or two bars on or near Paisley Road West are favourite haunts of Rangers fans.

The following is merely a selection of the many bars, pubs, wine bars and clubs throughout the city.

An increasingly popular pastime in the city is the 'Subcrawl', a pub crawl round Glasgow's underground system, getting off at each of the fifteen stops to go to the nearest pub for a drink. It is advisable to go with a local especially since in some parts on the south side the nearest pub to the underground station is not immediately obvious, but it is a good way to see the different neighbourhoods and pub cultures of the city.

Chain/Theme

Like any major British city, the central area of Glasgow has its fair share of chain and theme pubs, with establishments from the likes of Whitbread, Yates and of course the ubiquitous JD Wetherspoon:

<u>The Counting House</u> (*George Square near Queen Street station*) formerly a flagship branch of the Bank of Scotland, you can drink here in the splendour of this old Victorian banking hall. Converted into an open plan bar by the Wetherspoon chain, it's popular with tourists and locals alike, with quirky features such as the bank vault now being used as a wine cellar.

<u>The Crystal Palace</u> (*Jamaica Street near Central Station and the Jamaica Bridge*) Another Wetherspoons establishment, good for evening football; and good place to meet up if you are heading across to the O2 Academy or the Citizen's Theatre on the other side of the river.

<u>Waxy O'Connors</u> (*Within the Carlton George Hotel on West George Street, next to George Square/Queen Street station*); vaguely Irish themed bar with its curious 'Lord of the Rings'-like setting. Spread over six bars, nine rooms and three floors. The premises is a fun place, with steps and stairs running up and down through the maze of rooms and bars, and a rather ecclectic mix of "tree trunk" and church gothic interior décor.

Whisky

Glasgow has many options for whisky, though many may not be immediately be obvious for the passing tourist. Here are some good starting points:

The Whisky bar in Oran Mor on the corner of Byres Road and Great Western Road has a large selection of whiskies. It's a great starting point for the beginner; if you make yourself known to the staff as something of a newbie, then somebody in here will certainly be able to guide you through the different regions and tastes.

The Pot Still at 154 Hope Street, a few blocks north of Central Station. It stocks over 300 single malt whiskeys (as well as other drinks, of course), and the staff really know their stuff. It's also an excellent example of a traditional British pub, with a great atmosphere.

Other great options are:

➢ The Ben Nevis, 1147 Argyle St, towards the West End.

➢ Bon Accord, at 153 North Street, near the Mitchell Library at Charing Cross, with over 230 whiskies.

Beers & Real Ale

Republic Bier Halle: (9 Gordon Street; off Buchanan Street 2 mins from Central Station) Quirky beer pub (as the name suggests), where beers from all over the world are served to you after ordering from a menu. This chain is quickly becoming famous for it's 2-for-1 stonebaked pizza deals, and its recently introduced £5 all-you-can-eat buffet midweek (the main branch on Gordon St will service weekends, but not the sister branches!) While the beers can be quite expensive, you'll be hard pushed to find better quality food for the price in the city centre. A must-visit.

Beer Café: (Candleriggs Merchant City; inside the Merchant Square complex) Wide range of local and imported beers both in bottles and draught form.

The Three Judges: (Partick Cross, West End on the intersection of Byres and Dumbarton Roads nearest Subway: Kelvinhall). Lovely West End establishment with a continually changing board of ales from all over the UK on tap as well as a cider. They also have a fantastic selection of imported bottled beers in the fridge and Frambozen on tap.

West Brewry Bar: (Glasgow Green, East End in the Templeton Building). A Restaurant and micro brewery serving traditional food and German style lager beers.

Pivo Pivo: (Waterloo Street). This bar has a very good selection of beers both on tap and bottled. It is also popular for live music as well. Just round the corner for hope street and they proudly don't sell Tennent's.

Other Real Ale bars can be found at the Bon Accord on Charing X, Clockwork BeerCo near Hampden Park, and also The Three Judges on the Dumbarton Road, at the bottom of Byres Road, which has won the CAMRA award (Campaign For Real Ale) most years for the past 2 decades. Also check out The State off Sauchiehall Street is a similarly good ale venue and a cosy proper pub if you're sick of trendy bars.

Student

The city's large student population means there are no shortage of student bars, with large concentrations around the Merchant City area (for nearby Strathclyde and Glasgow Caledonian universities, as well as several nearby colleges), and of course Byres Road and Ashton Lane in the West End for Glasgow University. Another cluster (near Glasgow School of Art) exists along the western reaches of Sauchiehall Street, just beyond the pedestrianised section. Some of the most popular student bars are:

The Ark (North Frederick Street close to George Square) and The Hall (457 Sauchiehall Street - rail: Charing Cross, Subway: St. George's Cross), catering for Strathclyde/Caledonian Universities and Glasgow School of Art respectively were originally both part of the now-defunct Scream chain, but are now independent.

Strathclyde University Union (90 John Street, Merchant City short walk from George Square) Notable for once being officially Scotland's largest pub with 6 bars spread over 10 levels. Entry: £2 for non-members (NUS cardholders - entry fees for event nights may vary, and may be restricted to Strathclyde students)

Glasgow University Union / Queen Margaret Union (GUU at the bottom of University Avenue nr the junction with Kelvin Way, QM University Gardens at the top of Ashton Lane) The University of Glasgow's two official student unions are very different, from the "establishment" GUU to the more quirky and laid back QM. Open to matriculating students from any one of the city's three universities.

Nice N Sleazy . (421 Sauchiehall Street nearest railway: Charing Cross) A great student institution known locally as "Sleazy's" it's a favourite among Glasgow School of Art students, it's a cross between a bar and a nightclub, and even a coffee shop by day - one of Glasgow's best established student venues. Live music in the evenings, and just across the road from the seminal Garage nightclub.

ClubClassBus This converted double decker bus with fancy sofa style seating, fancy sound system and Led lighting, visits 3 great central bars on its tour of Glasgow, ending up at one of Glasgow's top nightclubs. It is a great format for Students as well as groups just out to have a great night out. Pre-booking is essential with the tours running most Fridays and Saturdays.

Style

Bath Street has a constantly shifting array of "style bars", which become more numerous as you walk up towards the financial district on Blythswood Hill. The quality varies wildly depending on your taste and tolerance. Some of the best are:

Bar Buddha: (408 Sauchiehall Street) The original branch on St. Vincent Street is now closed - and mourned by its fans for being arguably far more atmospheric than its successor, but still a quirky style bar with bags of character.

Corinthian: (Ingram Street Merchant City nearest railway: Queen Street) Wickedly pretentious bar/restaurant converted from and old bank in the centre of Glasgow's designer shop district with beautifully restored interior fittings. Food served is of a high standard, although drinks can be expensive. Note that a dress code (smart/casual - no sports footwear) is strictly enforced after 6PM.

Hummingbird: (186 Bath Street) Newly opened bar/club/restaurant with extremely stylish, avant-garde decor and 4 floors.

Bunker: (on the corner of Hope Street and Bath Street) Popular bar with office workers from the nearby financial area, and a good base to start a night out from.

Kushion: (158-166 Bath Street; nearest rail - Charing Cross) Mterrenean basement theme bar, restaurant and nightclub. Close to King Tut's Wah Wah Hut. Student friendly.

Gastropubs

Apart from Stravaigin and Brel in the West End (see the Restaurant section above), there are a few gems in and around the city centre.

Strata: (At the southern end of Queen Street, near Argyle Street) Award winning gastropub split over two levels. Well known for its cocktail bar.

Babbity Bowsters: (16-18 Blackfriars Street Merchant City; nearest railway - High Street) Notable for its fine range of imported lagers, the bar meals are excellent. You can even sit outside in the quaint little beer garden (when it is not raining)

Culture and music

If you like your rock and metal music, try The Solid Rock Cafe at the bottom of Hope street and Rufus T.Firefly's near the top of Hope street.

If you would like a taste the real Glasgow and experience a part of the culture few outsiders are privy to, try one of the many unofficial national drinks favored and savored by the Scots. This is probably the second (Whisky being the first) most influential, but no less important, drink that has graced the fine lands that comprise Glasgow and in fact, the whole of Scotland. This is the one and only Buckfast Tonic Wine. Known by many pseudonyms Bucky, Tonic, Sauce or Wreck the Hoose Juice.

The most traditional manner of consuming this beverage is by gathering in a park and pouring it down your neck before the 'Polis' come or by amassing a group of like minded individuals and wandering down a quiet cycle path in the dark, preferably when it's raining. There are a few regional variations of consumption as well, some groups mix their Buckfast with Milk creating an otherworldly concoction known as a "Buck-shake" or some times "Buck-kakke". Some add caffeinated soft drinks, further adding to the caffeine content of the wine. Though these are some of the traditional ways to consume "The Tonic" by far the most common way people choose to consume their wine is to sit in a flat or garden on a rare nice day, with their pals, with a bottle each (at least) and drink it straight from the bottle.

Traditional/Local

As the city centre and West End's bars become ever more sanitized, off-the-peg and tourist-oriented, finding a traditional "boozer" in Glasgow is getting harder. For the tourist who wants to make the effort, they can be great places to discover what many would call the "real" Glasgow, the Glasgow where Glaswegians hang out. The other advantage is that the cost of a drink is often a lot cheaper. Common sense should tell you which ones to try out, and which to avoid!

The Horseshoe Bar: (17-19 Drury Street short walk from Central Station) Possessing the longest continuous bar in the UK, the rock band Travis used to rehearse upstairs before hitting the big time; as a token of thanks, one of their Brit Awards is displayed behind the bar. Billy Joel has been another famous customer of this establishment when playing in the city.

The Saracen Head: (209 Gallowgate near Glasgow Cross) nicknamed the "Sarry Heid" by locals, this old school pub (began in 1755, although in a different building) lies at the gateway to the Barrowlands area and the East End. Like all pubs in the area it becomes an exclusive haunt of Celtic fans on match days, and gets very rowdy.

The Scotia Bar: (Stockwell Street) One of Glasgow's oldest bars (established 1792). Famous for its folk music and 'traditional' ambiance.

The Alpen Lodge: (25 Hope Street). Great little bar with classic fast service and local banter.

Deoch an Dorus: (427-429 Dumbarton Rd). Friendly, food-serving community pub with massive televisions for sport.

Gay and lesbian

Glasgow has a lively scene which centres around the Merchant City area (the so called "Pink Triangle" formed by Revolver, Bennets and the Polo Lounge). The city is gay-friendly, which is shown in the annual "Glasgay" celebrations in October .

AXM (formally Bennets): 80-90 Glassford Street, Glasgow G1 1UR, +44 141 552 5761. 6W-Su 11:30PM-3:30AM. This venue is situated over two levels with all you could want from a gay club. Recently taken over by the same company that run the popular AXM nightclub in Manchester.£3-W,Th,Su £5-F&Sa.

The Polo Lounge: 84 Wilson St, Glasgow G1 1UZ, +44 141 553 1221. M-Th 5PM-1AM, F-Su 5PM-3A. The upstairs bar is tastefully decorated in a Victorian style and is a great place to relax with friends. Downstairs boasts two dance areas, one playing all your pop favourites, the other chart and dance tunes. The crowd here is very mixed. Entry Fee on Fri & Sat Night.

Riding Room: 58 Virginia Street, Glasgow G1 1TX, +44 141 553 2553. M-Su 5PM-LATE!. Attached on to the Polo Lounge, this newly themed bar is home to live cabaret acts most nights of the week and has a Wild West Saloon theme.

Revolver: 6a John Street, Glasgow G1 1JQ (Opposite the Italian Centre and downstairs next door to the 'Gay Chippie'), +44 141 5532456. M-Su 11AM-1AM. Mixed and relaxed crowd. Small and friendly bar with a great Pub Quiz on a Sunday afternoon.

Milk: 17 John Street, Merchant City. 7 days, early to late. Cheap and cheerful bar below the Italian Centre.

Sleeping

Glasgow, like any other major British city has a multitude of accommodation options to suit all budgets and tastes. Hotel prices in Glasgow are on average, cheaper than Edinburgh (which makes Glasgow a popular choice for staying in during times of high demand in the capital for instance the annual Festival/Fringe), although there are periods of volatility when Glasgow hotel prices also increase markedly for example high profile rock concerts, or major Scotland football fixtures, so it pays to try and avoid these periods.

The city is well represented by the major international chains such as Hilton, Holiday Inn and Marriott - and of course the ubiquitous budget motel chains Premier Inn and Travelodge - both have multiple properties in the city centre and on the main arterial roads on the outskirts leading into the city.

Camping

Craigendmuir Caravan Park: +44 141 779-4159. Stepps, to the east of the city, is probably the nearest camp site and charges about £12.50/night for a two people in a tent. A train journey from Stepps to Glasgow Queen Street takes about 20 min. about £12.50/night.

Stag and Hen

Accommodation in this section is Stag and Hen friendly and, therefore, best avoided by those looking for a quiet night.

Smith's Hotel: 963 Sauchiehall St. G3 7TQ, +44 141 339-7674. checkin: 11:00-23:59; checkout: 11:00-11:30. Warm and friendly family-run hotel set in an elegant Victorian town house a short walking distance from Kelvingrove Park. Bond system in place in which as you arrive everyone pays a bond and it is returned once the rooms have been checked and satisfactory. £30-35.

Budget

Amadeus Guest House: 411 North Woodside Road, Kelvinbridge (Kelvinbridge Underground, just off Great Western Road, M8 Junction 17), +44 141 339-8257 (, fax: +44 141 339-8859). checkin: 2 pm; checkout: 11 am. At the heart of Glasgow's West End, offers family run friendly guest accommodation and breakfast, in bright, clean and airy rooms. Wifi available at a small charge. from £24.00.

Holiday Inn Express Glasgow City Centre Riverside: 122 Stockwell Street, 44 141 548-5000 (). In the heart of Glasgow, a modern hotel with 128 air conditioned guest rooms, licensed bar, free hot breakfast and WiFi.

Glasgow Youth Hostel (SYHA): 8 Park Terrace (Catch the number 44A bus from Hope St. Get off at the first stop on Woodlands Road. Go up the hill at Lynedoch St and follow the road to the left. The hostel is on the right hand side on Park Terrace.), +44 141 332 3004. checkin: 2PM. 150 beds split into dorms and family/private rooms (all en-suite). From £13.

Euro Hostel: 318 Clyde St, +44 141 222 2828. Right in the centre of town. Has dorm beds, private rooms, doubles and twins. Starting at £10.00. Private rooms from £20.00.

Blue Sky: 65 Berkeley St, 44 141 221 1710. Hostel with dorm accommodation. Dorm beds and double rooms available. £10 to £15.

Bunkum Backpackers Hostel: 26 Hillhead St, 141 581 4481. Hostel with dorm accommodation from £12. No curfew or lockout, free linen is provided. Moderately equipped kitchen. Small independent hostel on a quiet street near the vibrant West End. £12 and up.

1883 Guest House: 58 Glenapp St (100m Pollokshields East Rail), 07775 832 461. Small friendly guest house 3 km from city centre, easy public transport and on-street parking. £25-40.

Beersbridge Lodge Guesthouse: 50 Bentinck Street, +44 141 338 6666. Overlooks the Kelvingrove Park in Central Glasgow, just 50 yards from Sauchiehall Street. Full central heating and a friendly atmosphere. All rooms are double with en-suite facilities, tea/coffee making facilities and colour TVs with Sky Satellite.

Campus Accommodation University of Strathclyde: 50 Richmond Street, +44 141 553 4148. checkin: 13:00; checkout: 10:00. These budget en-suite or standard (shared bathroom and toilet) rooms are provided by the university. These rooms are extremely popular for budget travellers. The rooms are basically for university students but are open to the public during vacations. The location is excellent and next to Glasgow Cathedral. The nearest train station is Glasgow High street, and therefore links to Glasgow Central and Exhibition Centre stations. Very handy for conference participants. Local supermarkets and restaurants are within 1/4 miles walk. Unfortunately the rooms don't provide internet access, and you may have go to either internet cafes, local pubs or chained restaurants to get access to internet. £36.50 per en-suite room.

Ibis Budget Glasgow: 2a Springfield Quay, G5 8NP GLASGOW, (+44)0141 429 8013. Ibis budget Hotel Glasgow is a low-cost hotel situated in central Glasgow. This Glasgow hotel puts you close to the shopping and nightlife of the city centre, 15 minute walk to the SECC and easy access to the M8.

Ibis Glasgow City Centre: 220 West Regent Street, G2 4DQ, (+44)1416199000 (, fax: (+44)141/2256010). Ibis Glasgow City Centre hotel is a stylish budget hotel, located in central Glasgow.

Moderate

Park Inn by Radisson Glasgow City Centr:e, 139 - 141 West George Street G2 2JJ, 0141 221 1211 (, fax: 0141 225 0021). Fairly central, the hotel offers amenities like Free high-speed, wireless Internet, individual climate control, tea and coffee provisions and flat-screen television. Enjoy international favourites and local fare at the all-day restaurant. From £66.

The Victorian House: 212 Renfrew St. Small Hotel. Beds between £25-40.

McLays Guest House: 264-276 Renfrew St, +44 141 332 4796. Guest House. Beds between £14-30.

Holiday Inn Express Glasgow Airport: St Andrews Drive, Glasgow Airport, 44 141 842 1100 (). Modern hotel, 2 minutes from Glasgow Airport, providing comfortable air conditioned guest rooms, free breakfast and WiFi.

Ibis Glasgow: 220 West Regent Street (Near Blythswood Square - nearest railway station: Charing Cross), +44 141 225 6000.

Glasgow branch of this popular French 3-star chain. £55-60 per night for a double room.

Jurys Inn: 80 Jamaica Street (Nearest Railway - Glasgow Central, Nearest Subway - St Enoch), +44 141 314 4800 (fax: ""url="http://glasgowhotels.jurysinns.com/jurysinn_glasgow"). Popular chain hotel centrally located near Central Station and Argyle Street. £70-80 per night for a double room.

The Devoncove Hotel: 931 Sauchiehall St. A non-too-modern hotel located at the further end of the street from the city centre. Double rooms, including Scottish breakfast from £25. Clean and comfortable, as one would expect for that price, but don't expect 5 star treatment! Buses to the city centre for £1.10. Double rooms starting at £25.

Swallow Glasgow: 517 Paisley Road West, +44 141 427 3146 (). Situated near the SECC and Glasgow Airport on the outskirts of Glasgow offering restaurant and leisure facilities.

City Inn Glasgow: Finnieston Quay, +44 141 240 1002. A central boutique hotel offers a restaurant, bar, meeting venue and events.

SACO Apartments: 53 Cochrane Street, 0845 122 04 05. Great alternative to a hotel and perfect for business travel; also a stone's throw away from a number of trendy bars and restaurants.

Mercure Glasgow City Hotel: 201 Ingram Street G1 1DQ GLASGOW. Mercure Glasgow City hotel is a 3 star hotel close to the vibrant hub and cultural attractions of the city centre. The hotel is near Ingram Street in Glasgow's upmarket Merchant City.

Splurge

Crowne Plaza: Congress Road, Finnieston (Next to SECC/Clyde Auditorium - nearest railway: Exhibition Centre), +44 780 4431691. checkin: 2.00PM; checkout: 12.00PM. 4-star hotel on the riverbank and next door to the SECC complex. Double rooms from £80-£90/night.

The Grand Central Hotel: 99 Gordon Street (Adjoins onto the side of Central Station), +44 871 508 8768. This grandiose olde worlde railway hotel - once one of the city's most prestigious hotels - has been recently refurbished and restored to its former glory.

Marriott Glasgow: 500 Argyle Street (Next to Kingston Bridge - nearest railway: Glasgow Central/Anderston), +44 141 226 5577.

4-star hotel in the financial district, with good access to the city centre and West End. Double rooms from £70-£90/night.

Radisson Blu Hotel: 301 Argyle St (On the corner of Argyle Street and Hope Street/Oswald Street, nearest railway - Glasgow Central), +44 141 204 3333. 5-star hotel located on the edge of the financial district and literally next door to Central railway station - noted for its distinctive copper facade. Double rooms from £140/night.

Carlton George Hotel: 44 West George Street (Next to Queen Street railway station), +44 141 353 6373. 4-Star Boutique hotel located in the heart of the city - on George Square and near Buchanan Street and the City Chambers. Double rooms from £125/night.

Hilton Glasgow: 1 William Street (Nearest railway stations - Charing Cross/Anderston), +44 141 204 5555. 5-Star luxury hotel in the centre of the financial district, with easy access to the M8 motorway and Glasgow Airport. Double rooms from £130/night.

Hilton Grosvenor: 1-9 Grosvenor Terrace (On the corner of Byres Road and Great Western Road - nearest subway: Hillhead), +44 141 339 8811. Hilton's other Glasgow branch in the heart of the

West End with easy access to centre and local attractions. Double rooms from £140/night.

Hotel du Vin at One Devonshire Gardens: 1 Devonshire Gardens (Great Western Road) (About 1/2 mile from the intersection of Byres Road and Great Western Road), +44 141 339 2001. One of Scotland's most exclusive hotels - popular with celebrities. Suites from £250+ /night.

Malmaison Glasgow: 278 West George Street (City centre, short walk from either Central or Queen Street stations), +44 141 572 1000. Modern boutique hotel located in a former Episcopal Church. Suites from £195/night.

Blythswood Square: 11 Blythswood Square (nearest railway Charing Cross/Central), +44 141 208 2458. checkin: "tags="". Brand new 5-star boutique hotel and spa converted from the old Royal Scottish Automobile Club headquarters in Blythswood Square.

Novotel Glasgow Centre: 181 Pitt Street, G2 4DT, (+44)141/6199001 (, fax: (+44)141/2045438). The 4 star Novotel Glasgow Centre Hotel is a comfortable and stylish base to visit the best of the city's nightlife & shopping and the SECC.

Stay safe

The emergency contact number in Glasgow is the same as the rest of the UK: 999, but the (newly re-organised) Police can be contacted for "non-emergencies" by dialing 101 from anywhere within Scotland.

Glasgow is like any other big city: it has safe areas and less safe areas, and the basic common sense rules apply. The centre of Glasgow is very safe and you should not encounter any problems. All of the city centre and tourist areas are well policed. During the day, the City Centre also has many 'information officers' in red hats and jackets who should be able to assist you if needed. Despite what its local reputation may be, being a Western European city, Glasgow ranks among one of the safest cities in the world. Glasgow does indeed have some very dangerous areas - particularly in some northern and eastern suburbs - where drug related crime for instance is rife, but these are well away from the centre and it would be impossible to venture into them unless you were making a conscious effort to do so.

Crime in the city centre is usually limited to drunken and rowdy behavior late in the evenings - hotspots include the southern end of Hope Street next to Central Station, and under the 'Heilanman's Umbrella', the railway bridge over Argyle Street adjacent to Central Station; and the western end of Sauchiehall Street which have large concentrations of bars and nightclubs. There is usually a heavy police presence anyway in these areas on Friday and Saturday nights to defuse any problems. The West End fares better, but be aware that the back streets off Byres Road and around the University can quickly disorientate a stranger unfamiliar with the area in the hours of darkness.

Although you'll see it being worn everywhere by the locals, if you buy any piece of Celtic or Rangers-related clothing as a souvenir, avoid wearing it in public as it can lead to confrontation - particularly in the evenings. Most bars and clubs in the centre of the city universally ban all football colours, regardless of team. In the past, there has been violent encounters and even killings with locals, so it is always best to wear them away from Glasgow. Either way, football shirts from any club have been banned in schools across the city. Additionally, avoid wearing *anything* green in the Bridgeton area as this, despite its close proximity to Celtic Park, is a staunch Loyalist area which has seen violence committed against people who were simply wearing the "wrong" colour, regardless of what football team they support. Similarly, try to avoid wearing blue or orange in Royston/Garngad as this is historically a Republican area.

Whereas prostitution/sex work is legal in Scotland, both 'soliciting' (ie prostitutes accosting potential customers in public) and 'kerb crawling' ('punters' driving or walking around obviously looking for sex workers) is illegal; so avoid driving/walking around obvious red light districts. The main trouble spots in the city have historically been the Blythswood Hill and Anderston areas close to the M8 motorway - a busy office district by day, but usually deserted in the evenings and on weekends. 'Running a brothel' is also illegal, so 'massage parlours' and brothels can be and are 'busted' by the police. If you are in a brothel/'massage parlour' which is raided by the police you may be taken into custody and asked questions you don't want to answer. Avoid such places.

For more information, contact Police Scotland. There is one Non-Emergency number 101 to contact the police wherever you are in Scotland for matters that don't require immediate police attention. For emergencies, dial 999.

Stay healthy

The UK's National Health Service (NHS) will provide emergency treatment for anyone in the UK, irrespective of whether they reside in the UK. In a medical emergency, dial 999 or 112. These numbers are free of charge from any telephone. For advice on non-emergency medical problems, you can ring the 24 hour NHS 24 service on 111.

If you should fall ill or have an accident, then the two closest hospitals to the centre of the city with an Accident & Emergency (A&E) department are as follows:

Glasgow Royal Infirmary: is on the north east corner of the city centre (just to the north of Glasgow Cathedral). The location of the hospital is well signposted on all major roads, and is just off Junction 15 of the M8 motorway.

The new Queen Elizabeth University Hospital: (nearest Subway: Govan) is on the site of the former Southern General Hospital and has replaced the A&E services at the Western Infirmary (west end) and Victoria Infirmary (south side). Also contains the new children's hospital.

Note that the new Victoria ACH (Grange Road, Langside. *Nearest station: Mount Florida*) and West Glasgow ACH (former Yorkhill children's hospital, Dalnair Street. *Nearest Subway: Kelvinhall*) contain Minor Injury Units to treat non-life-threatening injuries.

Contact and Internet

Phone

Glasgow's area code (for landline numbers) is 0141. When calling from inside the UK, you may choose to substitute just 0 for the +44 part that we list.

Internet

If you are travelling with a laptop then you will find broadband internet access in the rooms of most, but not all, medium to high end hotels. If this is important to you, check before booking. Alternatively, there are many Wi-Fi hot spots in and around Glasgow and WiFinder provides a register.

There are also several places that offer web and other internet access if you are travelling without a laptop. These include:

➢ Yeeha Internet, 48 West George Street (30 seconds from Queen Street Station), +44 141 332 6543.

➢ i-Cafe, 15 Gibson Street (2mins from Woodlands Rd, West End), +44 141 339 3333.

- ➢ <u>Glasgow Coffeeshop (SYHA)</u> -- 8 Park Terrace, 2 internet terminals available in the basement cafe of Glasgow Youth Hostel, non-residents welcome +44 141 332 8299.

- ➢ <u>The Goat</u> is a nicely appointed bar which also offers free & unlimited wi-fi access & has a laptop available for loan. Excellent bar food also available. Argyll St. Near Kelvingrove Gallery & the Museum of Transport.

- ➢ <u>Offshore Coffee Shop</u>, Gibson Street, beside the River Kelvin in the west end. Offers free wireless access and has good coffee. There is also an art gallery in the basement.

- ➢ <u>Starbucks</u> on Buchanan Street and other locations has free WiFi

Getting out

Visit Loch Lomond and climb the nearby Ben Lomond (the most southerly Munro) for great views. It is a 40-minute drive on the A82 road from the West End, and trains to Balloch (on the southern shore of the loch) leave Queen Street (Low Level) every half hour. Tarbet and Ardlui on the northern part of the loch are accessible via the West Highland Railway from Queen Street

(High Level) several times a day; Citylink buses also serve the entire western side of the loch throughout the day.

Take a boat trip outside the city, either on a powerboat or on the Waverley (the last seagoing paddle steamer in the world) . Both of these services go to many destinations throughout Scotland.

Take a seaplane trip to Loch Lomond, or even further afield

Edinburgh, Scotland's capital city, is 46 miles to the east of Glasgow and is easily reachable by public transport. Trains depart from Queen Street (High Level) up to every fifteen minutes, as does the Citylink 900 bus service from Buchanan Bus Station. Buses to Edinburgh operate 24/7.

The historic city of Stirling lies 28 miles to the north east of Glasgow - best known as the spiritual home of Scottish national heroes William Wallace and Robert The Bruce. A natural gateway to the Central Highlands, the city's famous castle is well worth a visit. Trains leave every half hour from Queen Street (High Level) railway station, and is easily reached by car or bus via the M80 motorway.

Ride the West Highland Railway from Queen Street to Oban, Fort William or Mallaig, perhaps the most scenic rail journey in the world.

Walk the West Highland Way from Milngavie (an upmarket suburb of Glasgow) all the way to Fort William. The scenery on the latter half of the walk is absolutely breathtaking and takes you through the heart of Glen Coe, generally regarded as one of the most beautiful areas of Scotland. Reachable via a frequent train service from Queen Street (Low Level), or via the Kelvin Walkway from central Glasgow.

The Ayrshire coast towns of Largs, Ardrossan, Saltcoats, Troon, Prestwick and Ayr are typically old-fashioned holiday seaside resorts. Whilst most Glaswegians themselves have long abandoned them in favour of package holidays to the Merranean, they all have an individual charm of their own. South Ayrshire is the spiritual home to Scotland's literary hero and national "bard", Robert Burns. All are easily reachable via regular train services from Central Station.

Take a day-trip to the Isle of Arran. It is possible to obtain through train/ferry tickets to reach the island. The Isle of Arran is known as "Scotland in Miniature" due to the fact it contains many features of mainland Scotland in microcosm. Brodick Castle is home to beautiful gardens and has a path connecting to path up Goat Fell, the highest point on Arran which offers stunning views of Brodick Bay during the summer (The Castle is located at the north end of Brodick, student discount available). The island is also littered with sites of archaeological and historical interest including many circles of ancient standing stones. Take one of the circle island buses to see it all. Watch your time though - know the last bus and ferry of the day, especially in winter. There is a beautiful bay with a castle in the middle on the northeast in a village called Lochranza.

Take a day trip on the paddle steamer Waverley . You can catch the Waverley at the Broomielaw on the banks of the River Clyde, just a short walk from the city centre.

Owned by the National Trust for Scotland, Greenbank House and Gardens make for a pleasant day out in one of Glasgow's leafier suburbs. It's a 30 minute walk from Clarkston railway station (catch the train from Central Station (High Level)). The gardens have proven to be an inspiration to gardeners throughout the world.

A short (30-40min) bus journey West-bound down the M8 towards Houston is a good day out. Houston is a traditional Scottish village steeped in history (and is nearby to both traditional leather tanning town Bridge-Of-Weir and upmarket Kilmacolm, home to many local celebrities), but its main draw is the Fox & Hounds Pub, home to Houston Brewing Company . You'd be amazed how many Glaswegians have made this same short journey to sample the ale and traditional Scottish beers of Houston! Several brews are available all year round, with seasonal specialities on tap depending on the month. Tours of the small but well respected brewing operation are available. This is one of Central Scotland's most well regarded brewing communities, and well worth a trip. Houston is well served by two bus companies, but watch out as the service back into Glasgow is around 11PM.

Take a hike up the Kilpatrick Hills. Kilpatrick Station is only a 50 minute train journey from Queen Street Station (Low Level) on weekdays and Saturdays, and Central Station (Low Level) on Sundays. The hills are huge and from the highest peaks you can admire Greater Glasgow from a distance, with views as far as Edinburgh, Stirlingshire, Ayrshire and the Highlands on the clearest days. The hills have their own stunning forests, valleys, lakes, streams and waterfalls. If you lose your way a friendly local will always be happy to help.

Detailed Guide

Sights in Glasgow

What to see. Complete travel guide

Glasgow is a city located 35 kilometers away from the mouth of the Clyde River on the middle-Scottish lowland on the north-west of the Great Britain. Glasgow is the third largest city in the country. The city makes up Clydeside conurbation together with surrounding villages, towns and suburbs that are located along the Clyde River. Among them are Greenock, Dumbarton, Port-Glasgow and many others. The number people living in this Lanark country with its center in Glasgow reaches 1.8 million of people. The name of this country means "green valley" or "the beloved green place" when translated from Gaelic. According to historians the name appeared already in VI century. In the beginning this was a small fishermen settlement, but during the development of colonial expansion of Great Britain together with Scottish bourgeoisie and industrial revolution Glasgow became one of the largest and most important ports and industrial centers of the country already in the middle of VIII century.

Nowadays Glasgow is a city of contrasts because this place combines the remains of the past industrialization and modern stylistic richness. This city was the second most important city of the British Empire with London occupying the first place. It is also considered one of the most impressive and unforgettable cities full of sights referred to Victorian period. That time was famous for the contrast between poor quarters for working people and amazingly posh emperor mansions.

In the end of XIX century Glasgow was proclaimed the city of the European culture. For decades this place traditionally raises interest and is very popular among architecture and art connoisseurs, as well as entertainment lovers.

In Glasgow is located one of the most visited cultural institutions in Scotland - the Kelvingrove Art Gallery and Museum. It occupies a striking historical building, which was built in the early 20th century and is a striking architectural monument in the Spanish Baroque style. Today in this art museum, a unique collection of works is collected, among which there are invaluable canvases by Titian, Botticelli, Dali, Rubens, Picasso, and well-known Scottish artists. Travelers who visit the gallery in the warm season will be able to stroll around the surrounding landscape garden.

A great place for a family excursion will be the Glasgow Science Center. It is a large interactive museum where visitors can learn about the most interesting scientific achievements of our time. In fact, the scientific center is a large cultural complex, in which there are several exhibition halls, the largest planetarium in Britain, as well as a state-of-the-art movie theater featuring interesting popular science films.

The most beautiful monument of architecture of the 19th century is the People's Palace, which has served as a historical museum for several years now. In it you can see the most interesting historical exhibits related to different epochs. Another interesting feature of this palace is an adjacent winter garden. It is a large glazed gallery, in which plants from all corners of the world are represented.

A visit to the oldest civil building in the city - the building Provand's Lordship, should definitely be included in the excursion program. It was built in the 15th century and was once part of the complex of a large infirmary. When the hospital was closed, the building changed its status several times. Today, within its walls is a historical museum, whose collection is dedicated to the history and culture of medieval Scotland.

The most unusual city attraction can be considered to be the Glasgow Necropolis. This historic cemetery is located near the cathedral. Today it is of interest, first of all, from an architectural point of view. In the territory of this cemetery there are about 3.5 thousand unique monuments. The age of many of them is more than a hundred years. There is a necropolis on top of the hill, from which a wonderful view of the city opens

Family trip with kids

Family trip to Glasgow with children. Ideas on where to go with your child

Glasgow has so many interesting sights, some of which is definitely worthwhile to visit with children. One of the best entertainment complexes in the city is Wonder World Soft Play Glasgow. It is quite large and is designed for children of different ages. It has an equipped playground for the youngest visitors, as well as various gymnastic structures and attractions for older children. In the immediate vicinity of the playgrounds, there are café tables where you can always relax and enjoy your favorite treats. In the center, there are a lot of slot machines and slides. Interesting entertainments and holidays are organized here for children.

With children of school age, you should definitely go to the entertainment center Climbzone Braehead. Here, various very extreme rides are equipped for visitors. In the center, it is possible to walk on the rope bridges equipped at height, pass various bands of obstacles or to learn the skill of rock-climbing. All entertainments in the center are carried out in special safety equipment and visitors are followed by experienced instructors.

Travelers who enjoy winter sports should definitely visit Glasgow Ski & Snowboard Centre. This is a wonderful center for winter sports, which will be interesting for both beginners and experienced sportsmen. There are equipped slopes for skiing, as well as special areas for snowboarding. For children, there are interesting playgrounds with inflatable attractions and various sports grounds. It is important to note that this amazing outdoor recreation center is accessible to tourists at any time of the year. There is no real snow in it but all sports grounds are very high-scaled.

The entertainment center Gambado, is oriented towards kids. It is characterized by colorful design and a variety of play areas. A huge number of slides for children of different ages, colorful figures of favorite cartoon characters, favorite children's dry pools and inflatable attractions, are only but a few of the entertainment available in this center. The center will be interesting to visit with children from one year old. Here one can arrange a wonderful family holiday or just enjoy active recreation in a cozy atmosphere.

Among the variety of entertainment centers in Glasgow, it is worth mentioning the Glasgow Climbing Centre. It will be interesting for school-age children to relax here. In this first-class climbing wall, training grounds will be found for beginners in this kind of entertainment, and for those who have long been involved in the art of conquering mountain peaks. Experienced instructors watch after all visitors of the center, so one does not have to worry about the safety of kids.

The amazing museum Glasgow Science Centre is operational in Glasgow and is considered one of the best of its kind in Europe. In this museum, children will be introduced to the amazing and interesting world of science, and they will be able to conduct interesting experiments, explore various interactive exhibits, admire the starry sky through powerful telescopes and even learn how to produce electricity independently by turning the pedals of a bicycle. In this museum, excursions are held for children of various ages, including preschool children. It will be interesting for adults who will have the opportunity to recall interesting facts from various fields of science that they studied at school, to visit this museum. In Glasgow, curious travelers and fans of active entertainment will be able to find suitable places for recreation.

Cuisine & restaurants

Cuisine of Glasgow for gourmets. Places for dinner best restaurants

Glasgow is famous not only for its unique attractions, but also for a rich choice of attractive gastronomic establishments. Local restaurants will definitely delight fans of classical cuisine and gourmets who prefer modern cuisine. Travellers usually recommend visiting a popular restaurant called Black Sheep Bistro. This is the place where you can enjoy Scottish cuisine in its classic version. The spacious hall of the restaurant can accommodate more than a hundred visitors at a time, so Black Sheep Bistro is a great place for families and large companies.

Charcoals restaurant dedicated to Indian cuisine welcomes guests until late in the evening. The signature dish of the restaurant is delicious curry. The restaurant's menu is updated every season. Several times a week here are held interesting theme nights, during which guests can eat unusual dishes. Fans of seafood will be surely delighted with food, which is offered in Two Fat Ladies at the Buttery restaurant. In its menu you will find several dozens of unique fish dishes. Visitors also have an opportunity to order dishes from classic European cuisine. In the evening Two Fat Ladies at the Buttery often hosts interesting entertainment programs and live music.

Fanny Trollope's is an interesting restaurant dedicated to the national cuisine. Every night its halls attract big and noisy companies that come here to relax after a hard working day and enjoy their favorite food. During the daytime Fanny Trollope's restaurant offers visitors to select from a special budget menu, so there's no wonder why the restaurant has gained a lot of popularity among tourists. Shandon Belles is an elegant restaurant that is a perfect place for various business meetings. The restaurant's hall is always distinguished by relaxed and intimate atmosphere. Dishes from English cuisine make up the basis of its menu. In the evening the restaurant attracts a large number of guests, so it is recommended to book a table in advance.

Fans of pizza and other Italian dishes will certainly fall in love with Roma Mia restaurant that never ceases to delight its visitors with excellent food and enchanting entertainment program. During the daytime this restaurant is always a very calm and quiet place and in the evening it often hosts various music concerts and performances. Among the local coffee shops we should definitely mention Trans-Europe. Here guests will be always offered a wide range of popular European dishes and desserts. The tables of the café are located on the spacious terrace surrounded by rich vegetation, which makes the meal here even more enjoyable.

The traditional cuisine of Glasgow is simply impossible to imagine without Haggis. The cooking method of this dish looks very exotic to many foreign guests. Haggis contains sheep's pluck stuffed with a mix of oat and barley porridge, as well as various ingredients like sheep liver and heart. Whiskey is an important ingredient of this dish. Haggis is usually stewed on a slow fire and then served with mash potatoes or a turnip puree. Despite the fact that the cooking method of this dish may sound somewhat repulsive, everyone brave enough to try Haggis is simply astonished by its unforgettable taste.

During a vacation in Glasgow, consider visiting a café that offers ever popular local cookies called Shortbreads. There are many different recipes, so the cookies can vary significantly in shape and taste. Even the simplest and most inexpensive types of Shortbreads have an absolutely gorgeous taste. Many travelers buy them as a gift to friends and family members.

Scones are one more typical quick snack in Scotland. These are small lightly sweetened buns that are usually eaten with butter and various fruit jams. Scones have a very pleasant taste and are absolutely not dry.

Don't forget to try oatcakes during your stay in Glasgow. Perhaps, the majority of travelers has oatcakes in their home countries or even eats them regularly. However, these two desserts only share a similar look. Oatcakes in Glasgow are cooked in a peculiar way, so they remain somewhat wet inside. Local cafes often serve oatcakes with milk.

Nutritious meat dishes remain an important part of the regional cuisine in Glasgow. All kinds of sausages and other meat delicacies occupy a special honorable place here. Local people rarely have a breakfast that doesn't contain Black Pudding or blood sausage. It is usually sliced into thin pieces and roasted on both sides. A traditional local breakfast that locals eat every day usually contains fried eggs, bacon, and black pudding.

Fish and chips is one more ever popular food that is eaten as frequently as Haggis and various meat dishes. Fried battered fish with potato chips is available not only in numerous local restaurants and bars but also in many food carts and kiosks located on main streets of the city.

More on Cuisine & restaurants
Food & Drink

Glasgow's eating and drinking scene is vibrant, with food and drink available to suit all tastes and pockets. Popular travel magazine, Wanderlust, recently highlighted the city's "impressive gastronomic scene". These days it's firmly part of the city's unique culture: coffee and cake while shopping, lunch in or nearby a museum, drinks before a gig, dinner in one of our exciting, diverse neighbourhoods and districts.

The city's food and drink is about experience and authenticity: keeping it real, serving it well. In Glasgow, that's delivered by our greatest asset our people. We want to help you uncover the distinctive food and drink experiences which will enhance your stay. After all, whether you're here for shopping, a concert, a conference, visiting family or an event, everyone has to eat.

Discover Glasgow's best restaurants!

<u>Modern Scottish</u>
If food and drink is the new rock n' roll, then Glasgow's well and truly rocking! The range of choice is breathtaking, with new restaurants popping up all the time.

Glasgow's lucky our chefs are able to source some of the best local produce in the world, including outstanding seafood and shellfish; unbeatable game and beef; Scottish fruit and vegetables and award-winning cheeses. Combine this with confident, creative restaurateurs, and you'll understand why Glasgow's culinary offering is imaginative and cosmopolitan.

You can taste traditional dishes, regional specialities and local produce, like haggis, shortbread, whisky and cullen skink. Modern Scottish cuisine embraces this but then adds a twist, so you might find haggis pakora or crab and cucumber cannelloni on the menu.

<u>Outside Influences</u>
Glasgow embraced the flavours and cuisines of the many nationalities of those who've made their home here. You can

literally "dine your way around the world". From native Mexican, American, Asian, Indian, Italian, Spanish, Portuguese and African influences, to name just a few, the choice is truly international.

Drink

Glasgow is the perfect place to lose a few hours whilst indulging in afternoon tea, cocktails, gin, whisky or whatever tipple takes your fancy.

Whether you are treating your mum or spending time with friends, nothing tastes better than indulging in a spot of afternoon tea and there are plenty of places throughout the city to where you'll find delicious afternoon tea.

Glasgow's specialist gin and whisky bars serve an impressive selection, alongside home brewed tonics, and Glasgow now has its own first craft gin brand, Makar Glasgow Gin, launched in October 2014, produced by the Glasgow Distillery Company.

Craft beers are also bang on trend. Self-confident Brew Dog, adjacent to Kelvingrove. Indy brewers, West, based in the iconic Templeton building have the finest lagers and wheat beers. At the Drygate Brewing Company you can watch the brewing process as you try one of their 24 different craft beers or, brew your own! And of course household name, Tennents has been in the city for over 450 years. Do a tour of the brewery or try out their Cook School!

On the go
Find an edgy venue and set up some trestle tables, or equip an old truck, and the art of 'pop-up dining' and 'feastival food' is born. The street food scene in Glasgow is as vibrant as ever with pop-up experiences across the city, making for a perfect stop-off during a busy day's shopping.

On a budget
Whether you're a student, a shopper, a tourist or here on business, why not take advantage of these great deals throughout the city? From pre-theatre menus to places where you can eat out for less than a fiver, there's something to suit everyone.

Traditions & lifestyle

Colors of Glasgow traditions, festivals, mentality and lifestyle
A rich choice of interesting symbols is one of main national peculiarities of Glasgow. Some of them have appeared just recently, while others have decorated costumes, flags and

emblems for many centuries. Thistle flower is the most famous symbol of the city. The image of the flower can be seen on numerous souvenirs. This symbolic image graced the local coins even five hundred years ago. According to a legend, in ancient times the thistle helped to save the country from invaders. Enemy forces could not pass the field overgrown with prickly thistle unnoticed. The Scottish army was attracted by the cries of the enemy and defeated the invader.

Solitaire flag is a no less known symbol of the city. As a rule, travelers enjoy buying it as a commemorative gift. The flag look like a white cross on a sky-blue canvas. For many centuries flag has remained the official symbol of the country.

Not many people know that there's also an unofficial flag, which is sometimes called Ferocious Lion. Yellow canvas is decorated with the image of a red lion - the symbol was used by the monarchs as yet in the early medieval period, but it didn't receive the official status. Despite the fact that this symbol cannot be used by all the other organizations and establishments, the fierce lion has become the main symbol of local football fans. You can see these bright red and yellow flags on all football matches.

Whiskey is a no less peculiar and well-known symbol of Glasgow. The national drink is also very popular among foreign tourists. Experienced collectors can spend days studying showcases of local shops and choosing excellent drinks for their cellars. There are even several museums dedicated to the national drink in the city.

In Glasgow, as well as in other cities of Scotland, is very popular a special kind of fabric - tartan, which is used in tailoring kilts and other accessories. Guests of the city often buy elegant plaid scarves and coats as souvenirs. During various festivals and national celebrations men can even try to wear the traditional kilt. When choosing gifts, you can often see an image of the royal regalia - a sword, scepter and crown. These characters are much respected among the local residents. These days they praise them just like hundreds of years ago.

Culture: sights to visit

Culture of Glasgow. Places to visit old town, temples, theaters, museums and palaces

Tourists should not forget to visit the historic district of East End, which territory is the location of several important sightseeing objects. Here you will find St. Mungo Church and the ancient

Tron Steeple Tower. Don't forget to visit the church's cemetery. This amazing sight of the early 19th century is the place where many outstanding political and military figures are buries. Nowadays the cemetery is a place of a great interest from an architectural point of view. The territory of the cemetery is also the location of beautiful sights by famous architects.

You can perfectly combine the observation of famous architectural and historical sites with visits to various museums. The Burrell Collection Museum is a very popular excursion destination among tourists. The halls of the museum exhibit a luxurious collection of antique furniture, pottery, art and jewelry. The collection of the museum is considered one of the most beautiful in the world. Priceless artifacts have become available for public only in 1943, when the Burrell family presented them to the museum. Fans of theatre should not forget to visit Theatre Royal, which regularly hosts ballet performances and opera concerts. Quite a notable fact - the modern cultural center attracts a huge number of young people. The theater is nothing similar with those stiff institutions that can be seen in other cities.

Glasgow Royal Concert Hall is a no less popular cultural institution, which often becomes the venue for numerous musical events. Here visitors can get to a performance of a popular rock or jazz band, or attend a classical music concert. Speaking of attractive museums, we simply cannot fail to mention St Mungo Museum of Religious Life & Art. This is an original institution that provides its visitors with information on diversity of world religions. Here guests of the museum can see an interesting collection of artifacts associated with each religion.

Car enthusiasts will be genuinely interested to see the collection of Museum of Transport. The large-scale exhibition of the museum includes hundreds of car models that belong to different times, as well as a collection of models of urban transport. A part of the exhibition is occupied by a detailed model of one of the central streets of the city. Museum University of Glasgow also exhibits a very interesting collection that will be surely liked by the museum's visitors. One of its halls is devoted to ancient coins. This collection will attract not only coin collectors, but also all curious travelers. Given the nature of the cultural institution, some of its halls are devoted to most striking inventions of Scottish scientists. This is only a part of the excursion sites that are recommended for visiting and that will surely leave many impressions.

Unique spots in Glasgow and near
Kelburn Castle

The great resources collected from the visit of the castle were enough to completely renovate the historical structure. Today, he looks excellent. The owner of the castle is Count Patrick Boyle, on whose initiative the original art event was held. The owner of the historical building takes a lot of effort to preserve the unique shape of the façade. The preservation of the genuine exterior of architectural monuments is one of the most important and inviolable rules of the Historical Society of Scotland

Year: 13th century.

The Kelburn Castle, located in Scotland, in the surroundings of the town of Glasgows, is truly fabulous. The castle, built in the 13th century, has been reconstructed many times over the course of a long history, and hardly rose among the other old Scottish castles until 2007. The last reconstruction was carried out in 2007. The facade of the old building should be renovated, but there was no money for it.

The local authorities have organized an original campaign and used the gifted modern graffiti painters for renovation. A few months later, a part of the facade of the old castle was adorned with colorful abstract painting. The best painters from Scotland and Brazil have worked on the design of the castle façade. After renovating in 2007, Kelburn has begun to attract a lot more curious tourists and became the world-famous landmark in a few months.

The great resources collected from the visit of the castle were enough to completely renovate the historical structure. Today, he looks excellent. The owner of the castle is Count Patrick Boyle, on whose initiative the original art event was held. The owner of the historical building takes a lot of effort to preserve the unique shape of the façade. The preservation of the genuine exterior of architectural monuments is one of the most important and inviolable rules of the Historical Society of Scotland.

Culzean Castle
Year: 18 centuries.
In the middle of the 20th century there lived General of the Army Dwight D. Eisenhower in recognition of his role as Supreme Commander of the Allied Forces in Europe during the Second

World War. Now, these rooms are turned into a museum, which is dedicated to his life and military career. In 2011 the restoration works were finished and now the castle is open for visitors. Today it is a good entertainment centre, there are held a lot of cultural events and exhibitions. Even more, the castle has a restaurant and outstanding souvenir shops, which are always open

Culzean Castle stands out from other castles of Scotland. It was built in the 18th century and resembles more a luxurious palace than a typical strengthen structures. The castle is surrounded with a marvellous garden. It has a lot of exotic plants, there were planted even palms. For a number of years, this outstanding castle belonged to the predecessors of the Marquess of Ailsa. Now owned by the National Trust for Scotland.

In the middle of the 20th century there lived General of the Army Dwight D. Eisenhower in recognition of his role as Supreme Commander of the Allied Forces in Europe during the Second World War. Now, these rooms are turned into a museum, which is dedicated to his life and military career. In 2011 the restoration works were finished and now the castle is open for visitors. Today it is a good entertainment centre, there are held a lot of cultural events and exhibitions. Even more, the castle has a restaurant and outstanding souvenir shops, which are always open.

Also, it is possible to hold there a private event. If you a wealthy man, you can celebrate there a wedding, an anniversary or a simple banquet. As other castles of Scotland, Culzean Castle is known with its mysterious ghosts. People say that there live no less than seven of them. Some visitors and staff claim that they saw a figure of a maid woman. The most popular and mysterious is a bagpiper ghost. It is rather hard to see him but it is quite easy to hear the bagpipe play in the castle almost every night

Inveraray Castle

The castle was built in 1771 for Campbell family. It was used by them for about a hundred years. The fortress has not only an original façade but also a marvellous inner decoration, some elements of which have saved until nowadays. It is believed that Inveraray Castle has the luxurious in Europe Dining Hall. The main decoration in this room is skilful wall and ceiling frescos. During the excursion, visitors can see a Gun Hall. It is famous for its high ceiling

Year: 1771.

Inveraray Castle has its own outstanding story. It was built in a picturesque mountain area in the western Scotland. The castle looks like a castle in a Gothic style than a fortress. Tourists and locals like to walk in the nearby area. The main material for the building was chosen a blue-grey stone that was taken from the nearby quarries. The building is a good example of a combination of Baroque and Gothic styles.

The castle was built in 1771 for Campbell family. It was used by them for about a hundred years. The fortress has not only an original façade but also a marvellous inner decoration, some elements of which have saved until nowadays. It is believed that Inveraray Castle has the luxurious in Europe Dining Hall. The main decoration in this room is skilful wall and ceiling frescos. During the excursion, visitors can see a Gun Hall. It is famous for its high ceiling.

The palace has a great collection of art pieces. There are presented the original antique furniture, various paintings, sculptures and other interior decoration things. Not so far from the castle has placed a popular Loch Fyne Lake. There are usually held sailing competitions. The lakeshore has special places for fishing. The picturesque outskirts of the castle are quite popular among outdoor enthusiasts

Attractions & nightlife

City break in Glasgow. Active leisure ideas for Glasgow attractions, recreation and nightlife

Glasgow is a paradise for fans of outdoor recreation. The city is home to 70 beautiful parks and gardens, each of which is certainly able to surprise its visitors with original design, widest choice of beautiful flowers and exotic plants. The oldest park of the city is called Glasgow Green. It was founded in the beginning of the 15th century. Nowadays Glasgow Green has become a regular venue for various cultural events and national holidays. The park is also home to many interesting attractions. Rest in this park is particularly pleasant on a hot day as Glasgow Green is equipped with a large area for picnics. There are also playgrounds for children.

Rare plants and flowers can be seen in Glasgow Botanic Garden, which was opened in the beginning of the 19th century. The garden has become home to a rich collection of orchids and begonias. The greenhouses located here were constructed right after the opening of the garden. The magnificent greenhouses are adorned with incredible sculptures, which are the result of work of the best artists of past centuries. Victorian Kelvingrove Park is a no less attractive place. The park has become a favorite vacation spot of both locals and tourists. It is perfect for various outdoor activities. The park has special bike lanes, sports fields, playgrounds and entertaining attractions for children.

In addition to exploring beautiful parks, guests usually enjoy making walks to popular local markets and shopping complexes. Buchanan Galleries is a popular shopping center of Glasgow, which features a rich choice of boutiques and shopping pavilions. Here you will find a wide selection of clothes, accessories and perfumes by the world's leading brands. This is also a great place to purchase jewelry and attractive souvenirs. St Enoch Centre supermarket is also worth making a visit. Besides rich choice of products this place is an important architectural landmark. The building has a glass roof and is the first structure of this type in the country.

Fans of energetic parties, contemporary music and dancing will be surely delighted with a wide range of entertainment options. Every night the famous The Corinthian night bar organizes numerous interesting parties and presentations, during which guests are welcome to try delicious food and signature cocktails. Not far away from the center of the city is located one more popular destination for night rest - Bon Accord Club, which will also please its guests with a rich choice of snacks, great carefully selected music program and friendly atmosphere.

Other Attractions

Parks & Gardens

Parks & Gardens: When it comes to being green, Glasgow really does live up to its name. Meaning "Dear Green Place" in Gaelic, the city has over 90 parks and gardens. So whether you're looking for a place for the kids to explore some of the city's beautiful green spaces, delve into the hidden gardens or simply somewhere to escape from the city buzz, you'll be spoilt for choice.

Glasgow Green: A stone's throw away from the city centre is the historic Glasgow Green located in the East of the city. Glasgow Green is the city's oldest park, where you'll find the spectacular Doulton Fountain, the largest terracotta fountain in the world, and the beautiful McLennan Arch. Set within Glasgow Green you will find the People's Palace, dedicated to social history of Glasgow and its people. Adjacent is the Winter Gardens, venture into the elegant glasshouse brimming with exotic tropical palms and plants.

Cuningar Loop: Cuningar Loop is a new addition to Glasgow's East neighbourhood 15 hectares of derelict land to the East of Glasgow has been transformed into a fantastic woodland park as part of the Legacy 2014 project. Equipped with adventure play facilities, a bike skills area and Scotland's first outdoor bouldering park, Cuningar Loop has plenty to keep locals and visitors of all ages entertained!

Kelvingrove Park: If you're in the west of the city, you won't have to look further than Kelvingrove Park, with its River Kelvin walkway. A classic example of a Victorian Park, its setting on the banks of the river complements the many magnificent buildings which surround it, including the renowned Kelvingrove Art Gallery and Museum and the University of Glasgow. The park also boasts the magnificent Kelvingrove Bandstand and Amphitheatre, an amazing open-air arts venue in the city. Also located in the city's West neighbourhood is the Botanic Gardens, a tranquil blend of formal gardens and woodland walks, with the addition of the beautiful Kibble Palace glasshouse to have a stroll in.

Pollok Country Park: The largest park in Glasgow, and the only Country Park, is south of the Clyde. Standing in the middle of the award-winning Pollok Country Park, you would never believe you were only three miles from the city centre! Take in a woodland walk or get your wellies on and take in a Heritage Trail who knows what you will discover. You will also find a playground and orienteering, the ideal activities for the little explorers out there. You will also spot some Highland cattle and mountain bike circuits, all adding to the stunning surroundings of Pollok House.

Victoria Park: Victoria Park, located in the west of the city, is one of Glasgow's prettiest parks. It boasts an extensive range of formal floral displays, carpet bedding and hollies. Within Victoria Park is Fossil Grove, housing the remnants of an ancient forest, the fossilized tree stumps are thought to be around 330 million years old - Fossil Grove is one of the most famous in-situ carboniferous forest examples in the world!

Tollcross Park: If you're looking for something to entertain the kids, a visit Tollcross Park in the East of the city is perfect. Complete with a children's farm within the courtyard complex, regulars in the farm are Shire Horses, Shetland Ponies, aviary, rabbits, sheep, Highland Cattle and much more! Also located within Tollcross Park is the internationally renowned rose garden, with a staggering 240 varieties of rose all arranged in the perfect shape of a rosebud.

Queen's Park: Found on the south side of Glasgow is Queen's Park. With incredible views of the city from the flagpole, you'll be able to see the Campsie Fells and Ben Lomond on a clear day. The park also features also a flourishing rose garden.

City Centre Mural Trail

So let's take a look at where you can find these huge splashes of colour in the city, and how they've been brightening up local areas as well as supporting local artists by providing a space for their unique creations.

The World's Most Economical Taxi: You'll find this fantastical floating taxi on Mitchell Street adjacent to Glasgow's Style Mile, created by artist Rogue-one. Capturing the attention of all who walk past, it's a great piece to start off your trail.

The Barras Pirate : Head to the East End to check out one of the newer murals which appeared as part of the launch of the courtyard space at Barras Art and Design. 'The Barras Pirate', created by Rogue-one, is actually six year old Lola from Glasgow.

Billy Connolly: Created to mark the 75th birthday of the much-loved Glaswegian comedian Billy Connolly, you'll find three brilliant murals around the city created from original pieces of artwork. Jack Vettriano, John Byrne, and Rachael Maclean were commissioned to portray the Big Yin in their own respective styles and we think you'll agree that the end results are an amazing tribute to one of the greatest comedians of all time!

A Study of a Woman in Black : Not too far from one of the Billy Connolly murals, at the Saltmarket (near The Briggait), you will find this intricate stencil mural by James Klinge (aka "Klingatron") in his collaboration with Art Pistol. A study of a Woman in Black is an example of the intricate detail this artist displays in his amazing street art.

A Study of a Women in Black 2: James Klinge continues his trend towards portraiture and his study of the female form with A Study of a Women in Black 2. Found next to the grand St Andrew's Square, this companion piece to the above mural seems to beckon to the viewer, invoking mystery and intrigue.

Honey, I Shrunk The Kids: Again on Mitchell Street, you'll find this colossal image depicting a girl with a magnifying glass - catch it at the right angle and it looks as if she's plucking people off the street! Created by artist Smug, it's within walking distance of Central Station.

Glasgow's Panda: Did you know Glasgow has its very own Panda? You'll find this piece from artist Klingatron (James Klinge) at Gordon Lane, close to The Lighthouse, which is one of Charles Rennie Mackintosh's most famous buildings in the city.

Fellow Glasgow Residents: Take a look at the gable end wall overlooking the Ingram Street car park and you'll find all manner of Scottish wildlife coming from the spray can of Smug. You'll need a few photos to capture all of this huge mural!

Spaceman: This cosmic installation by Recoat and Ali Wyllie brings a touch of colour to New Wynd. Wyllie's work is inspired by comic book and graphic design culture, lending to his use of slick, clean lines, colour choice, and geometric backgrounds.

Badminton Mural: You can't miss this huge mural of Scottish badminton player Kieran Merrilees in the heart of Merchant City by Guido van Helten. Commissioned to celebrate the Glasgow 2014 Commonwealth Games, it now stands as a testament to sporting success.

Argyle Street Cafe: This installation by Smug on Argyle Street demonstrates what can be achieved with a little imagination, some spray paint, and a vacant shop front. The amazing attention to detail might lead you to think that the cafe is real if you don't look closely!

Big Birds: Designed to raise a smile, you'll find this fun mural depicting exotic birds escaping captivity on Howard Street and Dunlop Street. Yet another one of Rogue-one's pieces, you'll find it adjacent to the bustling St Enoch Centre.

Crazy Cat Lady: The latest from Rogue Oner is a feline inspired piece at the site of the former Victoria nightclub on Sauchiehall Street. A number of cats play and nap around their owner's feet, as she knits, whilst sporting a pair of cat slippers.

The Lost Giant: The Lost Giant is part of a series, which Australian artist Stormie Mills has created and installed across various major towns and cities all over the world. The Glasgow 'Lost Giant' is specially decorated with a scarf made from the Glaswegian tartan. The atmospheric character stands over the entrance to Sauchiehall Lane, adajent to the well-known traditional pub, The Griffin.

Tiger Style: You'll find this fierce tiger facing you on Clyde Street, designed by Glasgow artist James Klinge. As the artist's largest piece to date, it makes for a striking addition to the banks of the River Clyde. With plenty of space around the mural, there's no excuse not to get down there, get the perfect photo and add it to the collection!

The Charing Croc: Continuing the theme of wild animals, you'll find James Klinge's latest piece on North Street at Charing Cross. This amazingly detailed crocodile was created using multiple layers of hand-cut stencils, and it's the perfect addition to the urban jungle.

Charing Cross Birds: Right alongside the Charing Cross Croc is Art Pistol and Little Book Transfers continuation of their 'STALK' series depicting birds, foliage and fruit together.

The Swimmer: Another by artist Smug, this mural was one of the first commissioned to celebrate the arrival of the Glasgow 2014 Commonwealth Games. You'll find this huge mural down at the Kingston Bridge, cleverly placed to greet stopped cars.

The Gallery: Pop down to Argyle Street to see imaginative interpretations of famous paintings by Sam Bates, including Van

Gogh's Starry Night, Munch's The Scream, and Da Vinci's Mona Lisa holding a familiar soft drink!

Hand Shadow Puppets: This underpass at Cowcaddens has been brightened up by Rogue-one with his series of hand shadow puppets, presenting his masterful painting in the most unlikely of places.

Strathclyde University Wonderwall: Covering more than 1,000 square metres and several stories, Strathclyde University's Wonderwall is the UK's largest mural, commissioned to celebrate the 50th anniversary of the Royal Charter which conferred the University's status and also the 2014 Commonwealth Games. Read more about the amazing history of the University that the mural celebrates!

St Mungo at High Street: Glasgow street art regular Smug created this mural that can be found on a gable end on High Street. Depicting a modern-day St Mungo and referencing the story of The Bird That Never Flew. Fittingly, the nearby Glasgow Cathedral is the final resting place of Glasgow's patron saint.

St Enoch and Child: Just around the corner from the modern day, St Mungo is the complementary St Enoch and Child. This tender and detailed mural, at the corner of High Street and George Street, is a contemporary interpretation of the city's founding story; St Thenue/Enoch cradling her beloved St Kentigern/Mungo.

Musician - Sauchiehall Lane: Rogue-one and Art Pistol strike again with this fantastic mural of a musician, tucked away in Sauchiehall Lane. Sauchiehall Street is a great place to visit for new music, with plenty of venues hosting regular music nights.

Famous faces - Clutha: The Clutha Bar features a fantastic mural on the outside wall, celebrating many of the famous faces that have been associated with the venue. From Alex Harvey, Frank Zappa, and Woody Guthrie to Billy Connolly, Benny Lynch and Stan Laurel, this piece of art highlights the unique people of the city's history. Completed by Rogue-one, EJEK, and Art Pistol, find out the stories behind these famous faces on the Glasgow Music City Tour.

Charles Rennie Mackintosh: The trailblazing architect and designer, Charles Rennie Mackintosh, is the subject of a second mural at the Clutha Bar. The design by Rogue-one and Art Pistol Projects was commissioned by the new Radisson RED hotel to mark the 150th anniversary of Mackintosh's birth. The stunning design depicts the Glaswegian icon and his distinctive art deco and rose motif style.

Hip Hop Marionettes: Taking influence from the Beastie Boys and Run DMC, Rogue-One's Hip Hop Marionettes graces the side of a building at the corner of John Street, adding a splash of colour and humour to the otherwise plain brickwork.

Wind Power: Another imaginative image from Rogue One and Art Pistol, Wind Power, which can be found on Mitchell Street, was originally conceived as a live installation as part of Doors Open Day 2014. The mural celebrates the diversity of sustainable energy production within the Glasgow area and throughout Scotland.

Great Architects

As a proud Glaswegian and Scotland travel blogger, writing this article feels very close to home. Digging into my city's structural past and present, this is a personal look at what I'll always consider to be an endlessly rewarding element of Glasgow's identity and one that is being increasingly recognised and appreciated across the world.

All of my life I have been powerfully aware that Glasgow is home to some of the most atmospheric and memorable structures in the world. I started life in the city's west end and - after much jumping around - have found my way back to the place I love more than any other. The weather, the culture, the banter all contribute to that but, as much as anything, it was the enduring memories of Glasgow's familiar built heritage that pulled me home.

Here is my look at the journey through the timeline of some of the city's most diverse and evocative architecture and the geniuses behind them.

Medieval Glasgow Architecture

Examples of medieval Glasgow are now few and far between, with one fairly notable exception....

Glasgow Cathedral

The building is one of the best examples of Gothic architecture remaining in Scotland and is a reminder of a fascinating chapter in history. While the structure has its origins in the 12th Century, most of what we see today dates from the 15th.

Open to the public, the interior is everything you would hope for and more. Lavish stained-glass windows and atmospheric rafters that have sheltered centuries of worshipers surround the visitor. Explore a bit and you'll also find the tomb of St Mungo, Glasgow's patron saint, in the depths of the lower crypt. The best views over the cathedral are to be found atop the neighbouring Necropolis.

Provand's Lordship

Neighbouring the Cathedral is this, the oldest house in Glasgow. Dating back to 1471 you'll not find another building like it in the city for a comparison. Thoughtfully maintained and preserved, the three storied house/museum is a wonderfully authentic look at simple medieval domestic life for city dwellers. It is believed to have served as temporary living quarters for Cathedral staff before later becoming home to one of the canons of the cathedral chapter. This individual was to become known as the Lord of Provan, which is where the name originates. Much of the furniture on display today was donated by that king of collections, Sir William Burrell. The museum is free to enter for visitors

Glasgow's Great Architects

Charles Rennie Mackintosh (1868-1928)

One of the most famous names in Scottish history, this son of Glasgow left an eternal legacy on the city with his extensive range of design genius that still pulls in visitors in droves. A multi-talented architect, designer and artist Mackintosh contributed both to the shell of his buildings and the interior designs. Everything from furniture to structural decoration could be attributed to his creativity. Wherever you go in Glasgow, look out for his distinctive tall, thin typeface. You'll find that he's never far away.

Often collaborating with his wife Margaret Macdonald, their work can be studied and appreciated in numerous locations. With tributes in Kelvingrove Art Gallery and Museum, the Hunterian Museum and The Lighthouse as well as recreations throughout Glasgow, there are plenty of options for followers. In terms of his architectural legacy though, the following should not be missed.

Glasgow School of Art

Following a major fire in the Mackintosh Building on the 15 June 2018, The Glasgow School of Art visitor centre, shop and exhibition spaces in the neighbouring Reid building are currently closed to visitors. Mackintosh at the GSA Tours and Mackintosh's Glasgow Walking Tours will cease to operate during this closure period.

Mackintosh Queen's Cross

I was surprised to learn that this gem (not five minutes from where I live) is the only finished church designed by Mackintosh. One of the most serene locations in the city, there isn't a finer spot to reflect on Mackintosh's genius. It is also the HQ of the Charles Rennie Mackintosh Society. It is open to visitors all year round, although opening times may vary.

Nestled snuggly amidst the ubiquitous domestic sandstone flats of north-west Glasgow, the building is one you could easily overlook. But on closer inspection, there's no mistaking the style.

With simplicity a key element within his design brief, Mackintosh did utilise creative licence in his subtle and mystical touches dotted around the interior. The church chancel reveals several intricately carved wood symbols. They appear to show plant petals or seeds under the protection of an overlooking bird. It is a curious imagery that creeps into other elements around the church. And, of course, there is the attention-grabbing Gothic-style 'Blue Heart window' that dominates the hall. You can almost picture him pouring over his design scripts thinking how to keep the windows minimalist and discreet while also making them completely unforgettable. A truly great mind.

Scotland Street School Museum

I find this place to be amongst the most evocative in the city. Built between 1903 and 1906 it was to be Mackintosh's last commission in his home city. Immediately attention is drawn to the integral windowed tower staircases. Dominant and powerful they underline the importance of natural light in his thinking here. The interior is a combination of practical functionality (it was a working school after all) merged with Mackintosh class. Potentially bleak halls are sparked to life with glowing tiled pillars on the mezzanine level and the stark front-facing windows are delicately trademarked in his inimitable fashion.

It will be a jaunt down memory lane for many reconstructed classrooms and corridors of chilly tiled walls are sure to raise a smile. The museum is on the Subway line, just south of the Clyde and is open to the public.

Alexander 'Greek' Thomson (1817-1875)

So known due to his preference for Greek-style touches to his work, Stirlingshire-born Thomson's best work is largely Glasgow based. Although he never actually left the UK in his life, he read widely and used his curiosity and creativity to deliver structures that were as distinctive as they were practical. Pulling on influences from India, Egypt and Greece his neoclassical approach was tragically not fully appreciated during his lifetlme. But what is it they say about great artists? Many years after his death, Thomson is looked back on with enormous fondness by Glaswegians in particular. His legacy stands the test of time too, as his enduring structures underline his status as a man who valued sustainability.

Thomson evidently loved the variety and clearly thrived on challenging himself in the range and diversity of the projects he took on. With churches, villas, terraces, tenements and warehouses on his CV, there is no shortage of opportunity to appreciate the man's thinking. Two of his greatest works do stand out, however, and make for essential accompaniments to any discussion on Glasgow's great architecture.

Holmwood House

There is something very special about Holmwood, without doubt, the finest domestic structure designed by Thomson and one of Glasgow's greatest treasures.

This villa, in the South of the city, is often referenced as Thomson's 'masterpiece' and he has poured his love into every personal detail of its construction. Both inside and out the level of attention to detail is remarkable. Captivating in its pragmatism and with a hauntingly intricate exterior, there is an equally prevalent exotic feel to the tasteful interior. Superb use of natural light, including a fascinating and distinctive cupola set into the roof, are amongst the main standouts.

Holmwood also has an aura. Oozing atmosphere and rooms that just cry out for reflection and minds-eye thinking, the hustle and bustle of family and business life here is not hard to imagine. The villa was created for local paper manufacturer James Couper in 1857. Passing between owners over the years it is now in the care of the National Trust for Scotland. There is no finer place to scrutinise Alexander Thomson's mindset and legacy. Holmwood House is currently closed for the winter and will re-open to the public in the springtime.

St Vincent Street Church
Thomson's desire for sustainability and endurance is perhaps best shown by this magnificent city centre structure created in 1859. A bold temple faces the street, backed up by an adjoining clock tower. Tragically it is the only remaining Thomson church in Glasgow but is one that offers great insight into his style.

Even being set amidst the city's bustling business and nightlife centre, there is something ominously powerful about its temple-like grandeur.

William Young (1843-1900)

Glasgow City Chambers

For many visitors to the city, exiting from Queen Street Station onto George Square brings their first sight of Glasgow. Suitable then that the square is dominated by one of our most impressive buildings. The long-standing home of the City Council dates from 1888 and offers an imperial feel from the outside. Paisley-born, much of his work was completed in England but he writes himself into the Glasgow architecture charts with this one gem. Solid and functional on lower levels, upper levels become much more decorative. An enthroned Queen Victoria and her subjects look down over the main entrance.

City Chambers stairwell

Whilst interior comparisons with the Vatican may on first utterance sound far-fetched, it is no exaggeration. Opulent marble and freestone dominate the two principal stairways; Spanish mahogany warms the Council Chamber; fine artwork adorns the walls throughout and the Banqueting Hall simply defies belief. The latter opens into a huge space and its warm colours and intricate detailing make it one of the most magnificent rooms in the land.

The City Chambers underline the desire to make maximum use of our best architectural masterpieces. As the working home of the City Council, there is a bustle about the place that seems fitting. Tours of the interior run twice daily on weekdays and are richly rewarded.

Edith Hughes (1888-1971)

Mercat Cross

One of Glasgow's most fascinating intersections, this junction has been central to the city for centuries. Dominated by the Tolbooth Steeple clocktower, Glasgow Cross sprawls out roads in all directions. You can still imagine the din of ambling trade carts making their way to town in times of old. On a less romantic note, the Steeple was also where the city hangings once took place.

'Mercat' is old-tongue for 'market' and this is where much of a Scottish city's buying and selling will have taken place. Glasgow's own mercat that we see today was designed by Edith Hughes. Britain's first practising female architect, this pioneer helped to re-create the long-since departed mercat marker in 1930. Its small stature takes nothing away from its significance resurrecting it to its 17th Century glory was met with great ceremonial delight.

Modern Glasgow Architecture

Staying true to the great designers of old, Glasgow's modern architecture scene blends purpose with presentation in the creation of buildings that are known and referenced by Glaswegians on a day-to-day basis.

Norman Foster (1935-present) and Zaha Hadid (1950-2016)

What I love most about Glasgow is its open-mindedness. With the demise of the old heavy industries - that had made it the Second City of the Empire - came doubt and uncertainty. Could a once great city lose its identity? Not a chance. In recent decades, Glasgow has re-invented itself as a vibrant and eclectic hub, with this status owing much to its renewed approach to outstanding creativity.

Talk to me about Glasgow architecture and, while I'll always think of the work of the above great artists and of the city's plethora of Victorian masterpieces, I'll equally reflect on the modern and futuristic vision that has transformed the Clyde waterfront. The site of on-going major regeneration, Glasgow's riverside is now home to some of Europe's most impressive neo-futuristic architecture. Never forgetting or replacing the old, this is a look at another chapter in my town's architectural journey and a walk down by the Clyde is a must for visiting fans of design.

The SEC Armadillo

Immediately drawing comparisons with Sydney's Opera House, this building has become one of Glasgow's iconic images since 1997. The SEC Armadillo contributes to a highly futuristic postcode that also includes the neighbouring The SSE Hydro (a gigantic flying saucer) and the SEC. The epicentre of the concert scene in the city, Foster's style is a far cry from the sandstone jungle to be found in the nearby west end. Tradition was not to be ignored however as the layered exterior design was created to represent interlocking hulls of ships a nod to Glasgow's shipbuilding past.

Riverside Museum

My parents owe an eternal debt to Glasgow's museum of transport. As a little boy, this was where I'd be whisked off to when my parents were at their 'wits' end'. Never mind going to your happy place in times of strife, I just went to the Transport Museum. Until 2011 the museum was located in the city's west end close to where I started out in the world. It is now rebranded as the superb Riverside Museum and is another stand-out on a Clyde wander.

Designed by award-winning Iraqi architect Zaha Hadid, any initial 'back-in-my-day' scepticism I may have had was short-lived and the museum remains one of Glasgow's best cultural assets. Housing a vast collection of vehicles from bikes to trams, it is a fantastic tribute to the evolution of travel. Such a collection requires an appropriate surrounding and Hadid's design is superb. Zigzags up top immediately draw the attention - signifying a cityscape zigzags up top immediately draw the attention - signifying a cityscape and waves on water. Hence the design brings together the city and the river, both at the very heart of Glasgow. The graceful Glenlee Tall Ship completes the scene, standing guard alongside the building and reflecting magnificently in its huge glass walls.

Post Neo-Futurism?

Who knows what the future will hold in Glasgow's world of design. Which next great mind will stamp their mark on the city's architecture timeline? Alongside Glaswegians worldwide, I await with interest.

Sharmanka Kinetic Theatre

The elaborate clockwork contraptions in this Scottish gallery create small worlds of whimsy and horror.

Combining automata, haunting lighting, and unique soundscapes, the Sharmanka Kinetic Theatre brings to life historical tales with whimsy and often ghoulish inventions.

This astonishing kinetic theatre showcases the life works of Eduard Bersudsky, a Russian-born mechanic and sculptor. With the aid of theatre director Tatyana Jakovskaya, Sharmanka (which translates from the Russian as "hurdy-gurdy") regularly treats visitors to shows of theatrical phantasmagoria, in which Bersudsky's highly elaborate mechanical exhibits lurch to eerie music telling tales of Communist Russia's often murky past. As each intricate pieces lurches to life countless tiny monsters and people turn cranks, or ride gears as larger pieces begin to move. Every cobbled together tower and fantastic airship is a small living world unto itself.

Although originally hailing from Russia, Bersudsky has called Glasgow his home since 1993. The center of this work is at the theatre itself, but his phantasmagoric scenes and contraptions often tour the world like a nightmare circus. The works of the Sharmanka Theatre can be seen in museums across Europe and one of their pieces also makes up part of the Royal Museum of Scotland's Millennium Clock.

Although conveniently located in Glasgow's bustling city centre, Sharmanka transports guests to a fascinating otherworld in which mute mechanical creatures are the narrators of grotesquely engaging stories.

Fossil Grove

Hidden in a Scotland museum is a copse of extinct tree stumps.

Discovered in 1887, Fossil Grove preserves the fossilized remains of eleven extinct trees of the Lepidodendron species within its building in Glasgow's Victoria Park.

The tree stumps, which are more properly described as quillworts (a variety of fern), were discovered during a quarrying process and were dug out from the surrounding sandstone and shale. The ancient arbors originally grew 325 million years ago in the area and thanks to the extreme rarity of preserved prehistoric flora, the innocuous group of stony stumps is a major research site. In fact the building that surrounds the fossilized remains is classified as a museum.

Govan Stones

Early Medieval stones sit on display at the beautiful Govan Old Church in Glasgow.

In the heart of the working-class Govan district of Glasgow are 31 early medieval carved stones, dating from the 9th-11th centuries, standing in the Old Parish Church.

The exact use of the carved stones and their elaborate decorative designs is still shrouded in mystery, but they stand testament to the power and wealth of the rulers of the lost Kingdom of Strathclyde. Many feature intricate interlaced designs and take the form of crosses or crossed shafts. There are also 5 huge hogback stones, massive monolithic blocks carved to resemble the backs of boars or hogs.

Britannia Panopticon Music Hall

The world's oldest surviving music hall was also once a freakshow.

Built in 1857 by Thomas Gildard and H. M. McFarlane, the Britannia Panopticon Music Hall hosted some of the biggest names on the Music hall circuit and quickly became famed as being the most popular place of amusement in the city. It was one of the first buildings in Glasgow powered by electricity, and the auditorium was one of the first places in Glasgow to show moving or animated pictures.

In 1906 management of the old Britannia was taken over by A.E Pickard. Inspired by the great American showman, P.T. Barnum, Pickard converted the empty attic above the auditorium into a roof top carnival, waxworks and freak show. Soon afterwards he also converted the basement of the public house on the ground floor into a zoo and renamed the building Panopticon which he took from the Greek; Pan = everything, Optika = to see, as the paying visitor could see everything from attic to basement for one admission price.

The Panopticon survived until 1938 when it was finally closed, sold to a tailor and converted into a workshop. Today the Britannia Panopticon Music Hall Trust and Friends of Britannia Panopticon are working to ensure its preservation for future generations to enjoy. As such the hall is now protected as a category A listed building and as part of the campaign the Britannia Panopticon is open to the public five days a week, with the trust regularly performing traditional shows in the auditorium.

It should also be noted that Stan Laurel made his stage debut here performing a comedy routine. The Panopticon hosts regular Laurel and Hardy evenings in his honor.

Know Before You Go

Britannia Panopticon Music Hall is located right in the heart of Glasgow so is very convenient for buses and trains. If you are visiting us we are easy to find as we are above Mitchell's Amusement Arcade and just east of T.J. Hughes. Remember that entrance to most of our shows is via the New Wynd, the small lane between T.J. Hughes and Mitchell's Amusement Arcade.

The nearest train stations are Argyle Street and High Street, but if you don't mind a 10-minute walk, Central Station and Queen Street Station are also conveniently close by.

Underground: the nearest underground station is St. Enoch. When you come out of the St Enoch Underground station onto Argyle Street, turn right and walk in a straight line towards Glasgow Cross. We are just beyond T.J.Hughes.

Buses: First Bus 62, 61 & 64 stop right outside Britannia Panopticon.

Car parking is also available at the St. Enoch Centre, Kings Street, Glasshouse on Glassford Street and the NCP carpark on Albion Street.

Duke of Wellington Statue

This stately monument has been wearing a traffic cone hat for decades much to the delight of the locals.

Maybe one of the most iconic locations in the architecturally rich city of Glasgow, the Duke of Wellington Statue has been harmlessly adorned with an unauthorized traffic cone chapeau since the 1980's and has become so beloved that locals actively encourage the victimless vandalism.

The statue, located just outside of Glasgow's Gallery of Modern Art and has graced the city's urban center since its establishment in 1844. However sometime during the 1980's, cheeky passersby began climbing the proud equestrian statue's plinth and placing a traffic cone on the Duke's head. No one is sure who started the tradition, but inebriated tricksters kept replacing the traffic cone each time the city would take it down. The image of the Duke with his bright orange hat became so common that most came to accept it as the standard look of the statue and it became a popular photo spot for visitors.

In 2013, the city of Glasgow began to work on a proposal that would have increased the height of the statue's plinth in an attempt to discourage the practice. However the Glaswegian public was outraged and formed campaigns to put a stop to the proposal. Outcry against the upgrade was so strong that the city abandoned the plan altogether.

The prankish practice does not seem to symbolize anything greater than the playful spirit of certain Glaswegians, but that seems to have been more than enough to make sure the Duke of Wellington's head will not get cold anytime soon.

St. Valentine's Bones, Glasgow

Glasgow's piece of the patron saint of love.

In 1868, a wealthy French family made a donation to the the Franciscan church: a small wooden box labeled "Corpus Valentini Martyris," or 'the Body of Saint Valentine.' The church sent the relic to Saint Francis' Church, in the rundown neighborhood of Gorbals, Glasgow. It sat there in almost complete anonymity for over a century. In 1999, it was moved to the nearby, Blessed St John Duns Scotus, where it has been given a place of honor at the church's entrance. Every Valentine's Day, it is decorated with flowers while the friars say prayers for lovers. It has even led Glasgow to label itself the "City of Love."

Little is really known of the real man (or men) behind the myth. What is known (more or less) is that at least two men by the name of Valentine (Valentinus) were known in Italy and died in the late 3rd century, and a third Valentine was located in North Africa around the same time. The two Italians were buried along Via Flaminia. As a saint, Valentine first gained real notoriety in 496 when Pope Gelasius I made February 14, originally part of the Roman festival of Lupercalia, a feast day dedicated to St. Valentine. The stories of the different men seem to have merged into one over time, with most of the mythology about Valentine being a patron of lovers, helping early Christian couples to marry in secret, only dating to the 14th century and the writings of Geoffrey Chaucer.

Today, there are no less than ten places claiming to house the relics, all around the world, including the Basilica of Santa Maria in Rome, Roquemaure, France, and Dublin, Ireland.

Tips for tourists

Preparing your trip to Glasgow: advices & hints things to do and to obey

1. Summer months are considered the most favorable time for a trip to Glasgow. During this time of year nothing will spoil your excursion program. Travelers, who expect to devote much time to outdoor activities, should not forget to take some warm clothes. It can be rather cold here in the evening, even in summer.

2. Glasgow is distinguished by an excellent public transport system. In addition to buses and trolley buses visitors can also travel by trains. You can also purchase a special pass, Roundabout Glasgow. It permits to use trams and trains for one day. The cost of this ticket is about 4.5 pounds. A bus pass is called FirstDay ticket and costs 3 pounds. This pass is also valid for one day only.

3. Bicycle remains a popular type of urban transport. You can conveniently use it in almost all areas of the city. Inexperienced cyclists should not make a ride to the central part of the city as the traffic there is very busy.

4. In order to rent a car you will need a driving license of the international standard, a passport and a credit card with the

required amount of collateral in the account. The amount of collateral depends on the brand of a car rented. You can reduce your daily fee by renting a car for a longer period of time.

5. Motorists and pedestrians should not forget that any violation of traffic rules with cause large fines. There are always big traffic jams on the streets of the city during the rush hour, so you have an important meeting planned for this time, it is better to use subway.

6. Streets and numerous parks of the city usually amaze visitors with their extreme cleanliness. Do not forget that any violation of public order rules with bring you large fines. Rubbish should be disposed in specially designated areas only, and smokers should pay attention to prohibitory signs.

7. Before you make a picnic in one of local parks, you should specify its rules in advance. As a rule, every park and garden has a specially designated area for rest and picnics.

8. Do not forget to leave tips in restaurants and cafes of the city. As a rule, the size of tips is approximately 10 - 15% of the total order. In some dining facilities service charges may be already included in the total score.

9. The best way to visit various cultural activities and excursions is together with other tourists in a group. The cost of individual tickets for some events may be slightly higher than for a group of people.

Shopping in Glasgow

Shopping in Glasgow authentic goods, best outlets, malls and boutiques

Silverburn is the city's most popular shopping and entertainment center. Among its many shops, there are pavilions of famous European brands, as well as stores that offer clothes and shoes produced in England. There are many shops offering household goods, large pavilions of cosmetics and jewelry. After shopping, visitors can relax in one of the cozy restaurants or go to a modern cinema.

In the historic center of Glasgow you'll find St Enoch trading complex. It occupies a spectacular modern building with a glass roof. You can stroll around the complex in search of beautiful clothes of European brands and lovely souvenirs from local producers. There are several grocery stores there, as well, where you can purchase goods of local production.

The most busy shopping area in Glasgow is Golden Z. It unites several streets, which are a series of trendy boutiques and specialty shops. In this area, there are many jewelry shops that wealthy tourists will especially like, and there are also shops with Celtic jewelry, where you can buy great ornaments for only 6 - 8 euros. Here you'll find specialized shops offering Scotch whiskey, chocolate from local factories and popular souvenirs.

Bat Street and Hope Street are the focus of the most popular fashion boutiques. A lot of original designer pavilions with clothes, shoes, and accessories can be found there. It is here that you should look for unique items of wardrobe, unusual handmade ornaments and designer presents.

The coming weekend is the best time to go to The Barras market, which is right in the heart of the city. At this place the market has been operating since 1920. The most popular national products and delicacies, nice handicrafts and antiquities are available here. They sell a lot of high quality farm products at attractive prices. During the warm season, a huge choice of fresh flowers and seeds is offered.

Glasgow has a lot of shops focused on amateurs of high fashion. Cruise store offers its customers a decent choice of men's and women's clothing from famous fashion houses. The price level in this store is quite high, but the quality and exclusivity of the goods fully compensate for the high price.

Ladies who prefer appropriate attire will surely like Karen Millen store. It always presents a lot of elegant blouses, skirts, and trousers, you can always choose an excellent business suit here. All the things are made entirely of natural materials. Despite the strict style, they look very spectacular.

Mr. Ben can safely be called one of the most unusual designer stores in the city. The store sells spectacular American-style clothes that were in style in the middle of the past century. Here, you can pick up many interesting things, the likes of which you won't find in other stores.

In Glasgow, you should pay attention to gastronomic shopping. Ian Mellis store is especially popular with gourmets. It was opened in 1995. The owner of this store is a real expert in the field of artisanal cheese. He offers customers cheeses from local farms. Each kind has its own unique features. A visit to the store will be no less interesting than a visit to the museum. Visitors are invited to try all kinds of cheese before purchasing.

Those who want to bring a real Scotch whiskey from their trip should come by Robert Graham store, whose choice of elite drinks is simply enormous. You can choose varieties at affordable prices, as well as a real elite decoration for a home bar. Besides whiskey, they sell a lot of necessary accessories, including beautiful glasses. There are also cigars, so men will surely appreciate this store.

Useful Travel Tips for Glasgow

I have always thought that my adopted home town Glasgow doesn't get the credit it deserves, as shinier destinations like Edinburgh or the Isle of Skye draw in the majority of Scotland tourists. So I thought I'd help to convince a few people to add to that million visitors and put together a list of 50 useful travel tips for Glasgow. They will make you want to pack your bags immediately and ensure your trip to the city is a winner!

Getting to Glasgow & around

1) Even if you fly into Edinburgh airport, Glasgow is just a 50 minute bus ride away!

2) From Glasgow airport it's cheaper, albeit slower, to take the bus no. 77 to the city. If you stay in the West End, it might be so

much easier with the 77 too, as the faster airport bus doesn't stop along the way.

3) Try to get your head around public transport, even if it is hard. There are local train services operated by Scotrail, the famous subway also known as Clockwork Orange; the third-oldest subway in the world and numerous bus companies getting you around town. All charge different fees for single fares, and tickets can generally not be used on two different services.

4) Always have exact change for busses not all bus drivers will give you change. Better safe than sorry.

5) I use Google Maps to navigate the public transport in Glasgow! It's usually pretty accurate with time tables.

6) If you want to bring some movement in, rent a city bike! Glasgow is part of the next bike scheme, so you might already have the necessary app from another trip!

7) Most of Glasgow however is very walkable especially if you concentrate your trip on the city centre, Merchant City and the West End. Check out this 2-day itinerary to get you started.

8) Private hires are cheaper than regular black cabs. These taxis cannot be hailed on the streets, but must be called in advance.

Sometimes you've got to wait a bit longer during peak times, but you can save a lot of money! If there are several of you it can even be cheaper to call a taxi, than to take public transport! Try Network Private Hire (0141 557 1110) or Hampden Cabs (0141 3325050)!

11) If you're looking for an AirBnB, look for places in the West End (Hillhead, Finnieston, Kelvinbridge, Woodlands), the Southside (Pollokshields, Govanhill, Shawlands, Strathbungo), Dennistoun in the East End or the city centre. Make sure you are close to a subway or train station, as they are easier to navigate and more practical than buses!

The best Tours of Glasgow

12) Not a guided tour, but a great route for a day out is the Mural Trail. It leads from one impressive mural to the next and criss-crosses the city.

13) Hop on the City Sightseeing bus for a comprehensive tour around Glasgow's main attractions. It's a hop on-hop off tour bus and is a great option if cow only have limited time in the city..

14) Glasgow is all about its music you can even do tours with Glasgow City Music Tours to visit some of its iconic venues

and stages. I'm going to try their Merchant City Music Tour in May, and can't wait!

15) For a tour like no other book the *Glasgow Central Tour* it sounds like a weird thing to suggest, but this is a train station with a lot of history!

16) Glasgow Women's Library offers tours around town telling histories of the leading women of Glasgow might not be something for a first-time visitor, but someone who's into unwritten histories will love them!

17) Tours of the City Chambers are free of charge!

18) The Friends of Glasgow Cathedral offer tours of the beautiful cathedral just east of city centre.

19) While most tourist guide books suggest that Glasgow is only interesting in the city centre and the West End, there is a lot more to see. If you want to get a more authentic image of the city, definitely spend some time in the Southside and the East End.

20) After the cathedral tour, visit the *St Mungo Museum of Religious Life and Art* and Glasgow's oldest building, *Provand's*

Lordship across the road. Both are free to enter like many other activities & museums in Glasgow!

23) Behind the cathedral lies the *Necropolis* a rather morbid sightseeing recommendation. While the Victorian graveyard is an eye-catcher in itself, it is the view from its hilltop that really puts this spot on your to do list.

24) My favourite view of the city, however, is from the top of the tower of *The Lighthouse*, an architecture and design centre in the city centre. Entrance is free, but you have to climb the stairs up the tower yourself.

25) Another vantage point, albeit a bit out of the way, is the flagpole hill at *Queen's Park* in Glasgow's Southside. From there you can even see the hills north of Glasgow and snow-covered peaks of the Highlands! The park is a prime spot for a sunny afternoon and the glasshouses in the back of the park make every day a warmer one.

26) You might have heard about the famous *Duke of Wellington statue*, sporting a traffic cone on its head since the 1980s. Behind it is the *Glasgow Museum of Modern Art*, GoMA which is always worth a visit.

27) Head west to visit the beautiful *University of Glasgow* campus and pretend you're Hermione Granger or Harry Potter in the cloisters.

28) My favourite place in the West End is the *Botanical Garden*. On a sunny day, you can wander the garden or lie in the grass, but it's the glasshouses that make this place the best place for a rainy day.

29) As you might have guessed, Glasgow is a very green city. There are parks everywhere. *Kelvingrove Park* south of the University campus is one of its finest, and the *Art Gallery* is as impressive from the inside as on the outside.

30) By the riverbanks of the River Clyde you can find the *Riverside Museum*, designed by the famous architect Zaha Hadid. It's a hands-on transport museum that focuses on the transport history of the city. *The Tall Ship* anchoring right outside the museum is also open to visitors.

31) "Glasgow made the Clyde and the Clyde made Glasgow" no trip to Glasgow would be complete without a stroll (or cycle ride) along the *River Clyde* to see its majestic bridges.

32) Another part of town, another park. *Glasgow Green* is the oldest park in the city and spans from the city centre towards the East End. *People'sPalace* at the centre of the park is a museum dedicated to the history of the people of Glasgow, and house yet another green house cafe. If you visit the area on a Saturday make sure to head a bit further into the East End to the Barras market. It's a real Glasgow institution!

33) If you like fish, go for fish tea! It's like afternoon tea, but instead of eating tiny sandwiches and cakes with your pot of tea, you get a fish & chips supper!

34) *West Brewery* is not the most conventional place to recommend, seeing that they brew beer after German purity laws and serve German cuisine but both food and beer are too delicious to keep a secret! It is also just across the road from the People's Palace, so if you follow my advice closely, you're already in the area.

35) <u>Finnieston</u> has repeatedly been named one of the UK's coolest neighbourhoods to call home and I'm sure the food scene of the area is partially responsible for this. There are restaurants serving cuisine from all over the world on and near Argyle Street (careful, there's another Argyle Street in the city

centre it's not that one!). Among my favourites have always been *Ox & Finch*, *Mother India*, *Ashoka*, *Shilla* and *Cailin's Sushi*. For 100% vegan fare head to *The 78*!

36) Another popular area in the West End is <u>Byres Road</u> and its surrounding lanes. Check out Dowanside Lane (*Hanoi Bike Shop*) and Ashton Lane (*Brel*, *Ubiquitous Ship*) in particular!

37) If I'd live in the West End, I'd constantly brunch in one of the cafes along <u>Great Western Road</u> *Papercup*, *Tapa* and *Roots & Fruits* are my all-time favourites, but I've also heard about a new vegan-friendly cafe called V&V. For more substantial vegan food, check out *The Hug & The Pint*, as I've heard its fantastic!

38) The <u>city centre</u> is full of restaurants to choose from, but I'd like to particularly highlight two of my favourite Italian restaurants here. One of them is called *Paesano* and serves literally the best pizza ever. The other is *Sarti* on Bath Street (although there are two more Sarti restaurants in the city centre).

39) Finally, since I've recently moved to the Southside, I should recommend <u>Pollokshaws Road</u> to find food any time of the day. My favourite breakfast is served at *Gusto & Relish* their vegan

cooked breakfast is amazing, but so is anything serves at *Tapa* and the *Glad Cafe*. *The Bungo* is also great for lunch or dining. If you're looking for authentic Indian food served in a family-owned, fully vegetarian restaurant, *Ranjit's Kitchen* is for you!

40) It's easy to meet locals in Glasgow. Just go to a pub, stand by the bar and someone will start chatting to you.

41) If you want to see a lot of Glasgow while getting drunk, do a Subcrawl, a pub-crawl via the city's subway! In total there are 15 stations and here are some suggestions for pubs to visit. I'd recommend to end your tour in Hillhead, Kelvinbridge or the city centre (St Enoch, Buchanan Street or Cowcaddens) as there are loads of pubs to chose from here!

42) If you want to catch a gig in a cool venue while you're in town, keep an eye out for the programme at the *Barrowland Ballroom*, *King Tut's*, *Saint Luke's*, *Oran Mor* or *Nize'n'Sleazy*!

43) Loads of pubs have free live music on stage during the weekend like *The Butterfly & the Pig*, *Blackfriars*, *MacSorleys* or *Maggie Mays*.

44) If you want to meet musicians after their shows, head to *State Bar* a lot of bands and musicians head here after playing bigger venues around Sauchiehall Street.

45) Two of my favourite pubs in the Southside are the *Allison Arms*, and the *Rum Shack* just across the road. Allison Arms has a great local vibe with a mixed crowd, and the Rum Shack is a rum bar with a great beer garden!

46) Finnieston and Argyle Street in the West End are not just good for food, but also for pubs and bars check out *The 78*, *Distill*, *Ben Nevis* or *Lebowskis*.

47) One special tip for a cozy pub with a wood fire is *The Belle* on Great Western Road. It's laptop-friendly (free WiFi), attracts a mixed crowd and is dog-friendly, so there usually is at least one furry friend to cuddle.

Some extra tips

48) There is a lot of *free WiFi* available in the city but not just in cafes and bars. GlasgowCC WiFi provide free connection in the city centre, but you can also connect for free on most busses, some train stations and subway stations.

49) The *Glaswegian accent* can be hard to understand even in relation to the rest of Scotland. If you struggle, just ask people to slow down and repeat what they said.

50) Don't be intimidated to ask locals for advice or directions Glaswegians are widely regarded the *friendliest people* in Scotland and are always super helpful.

Best Things to Do in Glasgow

Glasgow is the largest city in Scotland, situated on the River Clyde. Well known for its beautiful, thriving shopping districts and the culture that it has to offer. It attracts a large number of tourists every year. It doesn't matter whether you want to experience culture, food or shopping, you'll find something to fit your interests within the boundaries of this up and coming city. The slogan, "People Make Glasgow", really does fit the place, and you'll be having friendly conversations with locals and travellers alike there before you know it.

Journey with us through the best things to do in Glasgow to learn just how vital the history of the city was to make it what it is today.

Kelvingrove Art Gallery and Museum

Situated within the heart of Glasgow's famous West End you can find Kelvingrove Art Gallery and Museum. Standing for more than a century it was purpose built to be what it is today, with stunning architecture and a range of separate exhibit rooms. As a free attraction it really shouldn't be missed, and it's only a quick walk away from the Kelvingrove subway station, making it easy to get to. Inside you'll find more than 22 themed galleries, and 8000 objects to capture your attention. Go from seeing Salvador Dali's Christ of St. John of the Cross to seeing exhibits on dinosaurs and prehistoric mammals. Not to mention all of the beautifully displayed animals, and the skeleton of a stag who could make even the tallest of people feel short.

Shopping on Buchanan Street

Are you one of those travellers who absolutely has to go shopping no matter where in the world you travel to? If so, then Buchanan Street will feel just like home to you. It forms the central stretch of the city's shopping district, linking you to an array of shops in each direction. It's best known for the variety that it offers both tourists and locals alike, and most shoppers spend a lot of time inside of Buchanan Galleries. In there you can find everything from Hollister and Pandora, to Millie's Cookies and The Whisky Shop. Given that Scottish weather isn't exactly known for being the best, it would also be a great way for you to escape the rain.

Glasgow Tigers Speedway

Boasting a reputation as the only professional speedway team in the west of Scotland, these men certainly have something fantastic to offer. The season runs from the end of March through to the end of August, but it would be advisable to check the match schedule before your trip if you're looking to attend one of their events. You'll have a fun filled, well fuelled day watching them, sitting on the edge of your seats when it looks as if they might fall. Adults and children alike will enjoy watching the Glasgow Tigers Speedway events while they compete for their place on the British Speedway's Premier League table.

Bread Meats Bread

Since the opening of Bread Meats Bread it has quickly become one of the finest eating establishments in the centre of Glasgow. One of the things that has earned it the reputation it deserves is that when you go, there's no such thing as reservations there. Everyone is treated exactly the same, giving it the feel of a real family owned business, where each customer is kindly treated as a house guest. Don't let the name deceive you either, they also serve vegetarian options! Pop in for an amazing burger, and give yourself the choice between something simple like a classic burger, or their signature Wolf of St Vincent Street burger. They also now serve poutine, Canada's national dish, and since this there seems to have been a nice decrease in the number of Glaswegians suffering with terrible hangovers! So take yourself in for a lovely, family focused meal.

The Riverside Museum
If you would like to experience more of Glasgow's past during your time in the city, you certainly shouldn't miss the opportunity to visit The Riverside Museum. You can follow the city's subway system around to Partick Subway Station and it's just a 7-minute walk away. The subway really is the easiest way to get around the city, and with its loop system you're unlikely to get lost. Inside of The Riverside Museum you'll find something for everyone, while diving into the rich history that Glasgow has to offer. Everything from locomotives and vintage cars to an actual Stormtrooper can be found on display there. So, take a step back in history and walk through the interactive "shops" you'll be presented with, climb aboard the exhibits and have fun.

The West End
Considered by many to be the most beautiful part of Glasgow, you certainly shouldn't miss the opportunity to see the West End

while you're adventuring around. It's one of those places that leaves a mark on you while you're travelling, having its own independent character that can't easily be defined. With a beautiful mix of character and stunning architecture it houses some of the loveliest vintage shops, and alleyways full of small, intimate bars and restaurants. You can find everything from vegetarian Indian restaurants to small restaurants serving classic Thai food. It's an area that you will be wanting to find yourself in again and again.

Nardini's

Both adults and children will love the well-known Nardini's Ice Cream Parlour. Step through the doors of the shop that sits on a corner in the West End and you'll be struck by the sights of 32 different flavours of ice cream for you to choose from, all of which are prepared in house. They won the UK Ice Cream Championship twice, and use a traditional recipe to ensure that their ice cream tastes better than any that you've ever tasted before. You can get small ice cream cones to take out, or you can sit and indulge in a sundae. There are options your children will love, like the Chocolate Marshmallow Dream, and there are options that might just capture your fancy, like the Raspberry Snowball Delight and the Tasty Toffee Tablet. Inside you'll find that it's lovely and warm, so even if you're travelling through the colder part of the year, which is most of it in Glasgow, you'll find sitting in the parlour to be an enjoyable experience.

Glasgow Science Centre

Have you got children you want to keep entertained while travelling? If so, then this is the attraction for them. The Glasgow Science Centre is purpose built to both teach and entertain children, giving them an insight into the world of science and technology. Children under the age of 7 can use the Big Explorer area, where they can use water and operate a crane to keep a pretend cargo ship balanced. Or they can put on their own little puppet show under the sea, while having some fun with a musical shark and a giant walk on piano. If your children are very young, then they'll probably have a lot of fun in the soft play area on the bottom floor. But adults and children alike will find the planetarium captivating, letting your imaginations run across the skies.

Kelvingrove Park

Do you prefer to have a peaceful day out while travelling? Kelvingrove Park could be just the place for you, situated along the side of the River Kelvin, and set in 85 acres it provides an urban haven for animals and people alike. There's a possibility that you could come across animals as rare as kingfishers and otters, or as common as red foxes. You should expect to see red foxes quite frequently in the West End of the city after the sun sets, they're a common sight and will leave you well alone! When the weather is nice the park is popular with all kinds of people, from dog walkers to the students of the nearby university. Have a leisurely stroll, or sit down for a picnic. Maybe you could even take your family for an animal hunt out in the park.

Black Sheep Bistro

There are plenty of restaurants across Glasgow that will capture your attention due to the pleasant, family run atmosphere that they provide. But the Black Sheep Bistro is one that you should certainly put some time aside for. The cosy, traditional atmosphere will have you captivated, and the family favourites that they offer will have something to suit your tastes. They serve everything from battered haddock to macaroni cheese, and a selection of different desserts. But it is advisable that you book in advance first, due to the popularity of this place it can get booked up fast.

The Royal Conservatoire of Scotland

There are plenty of performing art venues throughout the UK that can boast putting on some sort of performance already every day, but there aren't many who can say that they facilitate more than 500 performances every year. The Royal Conservatoire of Scotland is one of the few that ticks this box! When planning your trip, you should have a little look online and see if there's something that suits your taste, with drama, musical theatre and pantomimes there certainly should be. You'll get to sit in a comfortable, modern auditorium with eye catching architecture and friendly, student staff who are happy to answer any questions you have.

Glasgow Cathedral
Most of the medieval cathedrals that exist throughout the United Kingdom are now ruins, so you should take advantage of seeing one of the last remaining great cathedrals while you're in Glasgow. It has been used for worship for more than 800 years, and has one of the largest collections of post-war stained glass windows. You can see the brilliant arches, hand carved pews and memorial pieces that are dotted on every wall. If you have an interest in architecture, history or even photography, then the Glasgow Cathedral is the building that you want to see.

The Necropolis
Sitting directly adjacent from the Glasgow Cathedral you'll find one of the oddest attractions that you should see during your

time in Glasgow. Modelled on the Pere-Lachaise in Paris, The Necropolis is now known as one of the most significant cemeteries in the whole of Europe. In the Summer months you can find an array of flowers, bees and butterflies adding colour to the 50,000 monuments that sit in the 37 acres of land. You're safe to explore for free, and you're safe knowing that Park Rangers patrol the cemetery on a daily basis. Chances are you'll recognise an area or two, as The Necropolis has featured in a wide range of television programmes and films!

Tiffney's Steakhouse

If you find yourself in the West End deciding where to eat, Tiffney's Steakhouse should be somewhere near the top of your list. Providing food that is completely sourced from local suppliers you know that you're getting the best of quality. Their Highland cattle are reared in a natural, grass fed environment, then their beef is usually dry aged for around 50 days. Sit inside and enjoy a beautiful meal, cooked exactly how you want it. Or turn up on a Sunday and have one of their famous set Sunday Roasts, a staple tradition across the UK.

The People's Palace and Winter Gardens

Do you enjoy learning about the history of each new city that you visit? Now as weather dependent as this attraction is, it will give you the opportunity to view the way life was in Glasgow throughout the 18th to the 20th century. Inside of the main house you'll find a collection of artefacts, photographs, prints and films from across the years. The Winter Gardens outside of the house are beautiful, which is what makes it such a weather dependent attraction, you can wonder amongst plants from far off lands, and see the beautifully restored Doulton fountain. If you start to get a little bit hungry among the grounds, then there's a fairly priced café where you can rest and have a bite to eat.

The Glasgow School of Art

You can learn a lot about the history of Glasgow from this attraction, which features an hour long tour. You can learn about the famous Rennie Mackintosh and his life, from being a student to a master designer whose work is known around the world. Unfortunately, the building did suffer fire damage recently, so it has had to be restored. The thing that really fascinates a lot of travellers about Mackintosh's work is his mind. He managed to work in a variety of different sectors, acting as a lead architect, a painter, an interior designer and an all-round brilliant artist. His name is known to the vast majority of people who call Glasgow home, and you can see why too.

The SSE Hydro

If you like to watch performances while you're travelling, then it would be more than worth having a look at what artists are playing at The SSE Hydro at the time that you're travelling. They've housed many a famous name in their purpose built entertainment venue, and with many surrounding bars and restaurants you'll be able to keep yourself busy both before and after. The venue itself is quite a sight, and has enough room for a large number of people watching the performance, but it quite often shows not just music, but comedy and a variety of other shows. You do need to be aware that it can get quite busy, but for most people this just adds to the atmosphere.

Tick Tock Unlock

Live escape games really have caused quite the stir within Britain over the past several months, with this particular venue giving you the opportunity to channel your own inner detective in a team. Your team have to communicate effectively to solve the puzzles that are laid out before them, unravelling the clues that will allow them to escape. Unlike a few venues that house similar live escape games their rooms are all quite large, making them safe for people who suffer with claustrophobia! The exact price can vary depending on the time of year, and you should book online to avoid disappointment.

Hunterian Museum

Adding the perfect dash to the already beautiful museums that exist across Glasgow the Hunterian Museum really is the cherry on top that finishes it off. With a mixture of permanent and temporary exhibitions you can see everything from Ichthyosaurs to Comic Invention. There is also a Zoology Museum you can enter, and both are completely admission free. Occasionally there will be a special exhibition, they cost £5 to enter. Get the Hunterian Museum added to the list of places that you want to visit while you're in Glasgow!

Pollok Country Park

As the only country park within the whole of Glasgow it has its own reputation. Add to this that it has won awards such as the Best Park in Britain, and the Best Park in Europe over the past decade and you'll know that it's worth seeing. With walking trails set among 360 acres of green land you will be met with the opportunity to see an array of animals, including Highland Cattle, up close. Children will absolutely love it, but they'll also be entertained by the great areas built specifically for children to play in, and the natural mini waterfalls that they'll have the opportunities to see depending on which trail you take.

Nippon Kitchen

Just as the Hunterian Museum is the cherry on top of the museums in Glasgow, Nippon Kitchen is a restaurant that stands up on its own right. Using specialist ingredients specifically imported straight from Japan, and fresh produce from only local suppliers you can imagine that their customers are always provided with the best of service. It provides a classic, minimalistic Japanese layout, set among beautiful wooden panels. Importing their sake from Japan they can give you a wide variety to choose from, and are happy to make recommendations for you if you're not sure. Whether it's tempura, ramen or sushi, you'll find it here.

City Chambers

Situated in the famous George Square the City Chambers act as the home to Glasgow City Council. You can take a free guided tour through the building at either 10.30am, or 2.30pm on weekdays, but unfortunately they aren't available at the weekend. From the outside of the building you wouldn't even get the idea to expect the grand inner chambers that lie within the case of the outer architecture. With a ballroom that appears to have stepped out of another century, and 2 spires with decorated dome ceilings. The tour guides all provide an exceptional service, telling you just the right amount of information to teach you about what you're seeing. Make sure you take a camera with you, you'll get some beautiful shots in there.

Glasgow Film Theatre
For those of you who love to see the classics of world cinema, or contemporary art house films, Glasgow Film Theatre is the place for you. It houses several film festivals a year, and you're bound to find something you might enjoy hidden within the building, be sure to look online for a full listing of all of their upcoming shows. They take pride in taking a personal approach with their audiences, providing them with a comfortable, friendly environment to watch the film in. You can also find everything from craft beer to cake nestled within the Café Cosmo area of their Theatre. So go, sit back and enjoy yourself.

Grosvenor Riverboat Casino
Are you one of those travellers that enjoys the occasional trip to a casino? If you are, then add the Grosvenor Riverboat Casino to your list immediately. Nestled on the banks of the River Clyde you have a beautiful view, especially as the sun is setting down

the river. Along with a their a la Carte Louisiana style restaurant they have a late night bar, and a comprehensive gaming environment. This includes roulette tables, blackjack, poker tables and popular slot machines. With friendly staff, you can either sit down and enjoy a lovely meal, or take your chance in the hand of fate.

Willow Tea Rooms

While everyone has different tastes, one of the two Willow Tea Rooms venues will be worth seeing while you're in Glasgow. Going back to the famous Rennie Mackintosh, he played a large part in their design back in 1903. In fact, he designed everything about them, from the architecture to the waitresses' outfits. While one exists on Sauchiehall Street, the other sits in the famous shopping area of Buchanan Street. Try everything from homemade sandwiches to traditional scones with clotted cream and jam. Not to mention the variety of teas and coffees that will be available to you.

The End

Lightning Source UK Ltd.
Milton Keynes UK
UKHW020635171120
373555UK00011B/593